SIMPLE GARDEN PROJECTS

ORIGINAL DESIGNS TO BUILD IN YOUR GARDEN

DAVID STEVENS

CONRAN OCTOPUS

First published in Great Britain in 1992 by
Conran Octopus Limited
37 Shelton Street
London WC2H 9HN

Text copyright © David Stevens 1992
Design and layout copyright © Conran
Octopus Limited 1992

This paperback edition first published in 1996

Reprinted 1996

British Library Cataloguing in Publication Data

Stevens, David, 1943–
    Simple garden projects :
    original designs to build in your garden.
    I. Title
    712.6

ISBN 1-85029-725-8

PUBLISHER'S NOTE
Whilst every effort has been made to
ensure that all the information contained
in this book is correct, the publisher
cannot be held responsible for any loss,
damage or injury caused by reliance upon
the accuracy of such information. It is also
important to obtain specialist advice on
plumbing and electricity before
attempting any alterations to these
services yourself.

Art Editor: Karen Bowen
Copy Editor: Rebecca Reid
Editorial Assistant: Olivia Aarons
Picture Researcher: Abigail Ahern
Production Controller: Julia Golding
Illustrator: Tom Lomax
Visualizer: Mike Trier

DIMENSIONS
Never mix metric and imperial
dimensions when you are making a
calculation or building a project.

Typeset by Servis Filmsetting Ltd,
Manchester

Printed and bound in Hong Kong

CONTENTS

INTRODUCTION
6

**PATHS
AND PATIOS**
16

Projects:
DECKING
28

BARBECUE
34

**SEATING
SENSE**
36

Projects:
TREE SEAT
42

ARBOUR
48

**DECORATIVE
DIVIDERS**
52

Projects:
GARDEN DIVIDER
60

BEAN SUPPORT
64

**WATER
FEATURES**
70

Projects:
RAISED POND
78

FOUNTAIN
84

**DIRECTORY OF
TECHNIQUES**
88

INDEX
94

ACKNOWLEDGMENTS
96

INTRODUCTION

Good design is all about simplicity, common sense and, above all, practicality. This is particularly true when designing a garden, as overcomplication is the death of any worthwhile composition. The trouble, of course, is that garden centre displays, press reports and a wealth of expert advice continually tempt us to buy new products and try new ideas, so it's little wonder that this valuable space around our home becomes a jumble of unrelated features.

A well-laid-out garden should fulfil two broad criteria: it must look good for 365 days of the year and must never be a burden, in terms of maintenance, to its owner.

With careful planning, you can produce a garden that is aesthetically pleasing and fits you in an entirely unique way. This planning starts with a simple survey of your plot, moves on to an analysis of what you need and finishes with the implementation of those ideas.

In this trouble-free garden, maintenance has been kept to an absolute minimum by the clever use of paving, gravel and planting. The raised terrace is a natural focal point, leading both feet and eye to a secluded sitting area.

PLANNING A GARDEN

The problem with many a plot comes down to lack of planning. While many people are quite happy to tackle interior decoration and planning, their ideas often tend to dry up as soon as they move outside. In part this is due to the confusion of all those long, Latin plant names, in part to sporadic binges at the local garden centre, when we return home with a car-load of goodies and little idea of where to put them all. But the real problem is that many of us still look upon the garden as separate from the house, a different environment for a different range of activities. As soon as we realize that the two elements, house and garden, are in fact one, the whole problem becomes a lot simpler.

For a garden to be a success, the layout should be thought about in much the same way as a room inside the house. True, it may not have a ceiling, but the floors and walls are just the same, and you will need furnishings and space for sitting, dining, play and other activities, as well as the growing of plants. Arches and pergolas are the equivalent of doors; overhead beams and arbours help to define intimate areas; while water, something that is little used inside, can be enjoyed for its almost endless variety as well as its cooling influence.

I have been planning gardens for many years and have learnt that, while the genius of creativity flares from time to time, the real worth of a designer is that he or she works to a well-tried and tested set of rules that the designer knows will be successful for any given situation that may arise. In fact, the whole design process is a sequential one and while you may have the glimmer of an idea right at the beginning, the initial stages are all to do with simple fact-finding and information-gathering.

THE SURVEY

Long before you start to work out what you want to see in your garden, you need to know just what features you have got to start with. A simple survey involves measuring the plot, noting down all the existing features and checking any other relevant factors that are likely to affect the actual design. For this you will need several sheets of paper, a clip board, a pencil, a 30m (100ft) tape

Above: *A great deal of garden design is about dividing a large space into a number of more manageable smaller areas. Arches and pergolas are ideal for doing this but should always be positioned so that they form a positive doorway or entrance to the room beyond. This arch does just that as well as providing a slight air of mystery by partially screening the view and heightening tension. Planting is the perfect foil to the old stone path, softening the hard edges of the walkway.*

Opposite: *In this tiny town garden the pattern has been built up by a combination of rectangular shapes close to the house and a strong circle of granite setts further away. The two elements are quite different in character but the broad step effectively separates them and allows the composition to work. As well as providing privacy, walls like this act as the perfect host for climbers, softening what would otherwise be a stark and uninteresting outlook.*

measure, a couple of bamboo canes or metal pins and a child's magnetic compass. If your garden is so complicated by steep changes of levels, awkward cross-falls and innumerable trees that you pale at the thought of carrying out the survey yourself, the modest fee charged by a professional surveyor may be well worth the time and trouble you are saved.

The first stage of the survey is to go into the garden and simply draw out the shape of the house and the boundaries to scale, showing the position of doors and windows, manholes or drains, garden buildings and any slope or change of level. The positions of any existing trees or shrubs should be noted, along with features such as paving and paths and the material the boundaries are made from. Next, take the tape and, fixing it to one boundary close to the house, run it across the rear of the building and parallel to it, right the way to the other side. Leave the tape in place and check the consecutive distances of all the features that you marked. The corner of the house might be 1m (about 3ft), one side of the French doors at 1.6m (5ft 3in), the other side at 2m (6ft 6in) and so on until you get to the other side. Once this set of measurements is complete, run the tape the other way, at 90 degrees to the first, down the garden and check all the relevant measurements in that direction.

LONG NARROW GARDEN

This narrow garden (right) has a length-to-width ratio of about one to five. Given the shape of the garden, one would normally think of using a rectangular pattern to link it strongly with the building, but here a circular terrace is particularly successful, the sweep of brick being echoed by the raised beds and curved steps. A path then sweeps away under the pergola and crosses the lawn before pivoting past an apple tree to terminate at the informal brick-paved sitting area that fronts a summer house. Beyond this, a gate leads through a high wall to the secret garden. Its hidden location makes use of surprise, one of the most important elements in good garden design.

KEY: 1 Gate; 2 Tree; 3 Secret Garden; 4 Mixed Planting; 5 Brick Paving; 6 Summer House; 7 Pergola; 8 Millstone; 9 Raised Bed; 10 Steps.

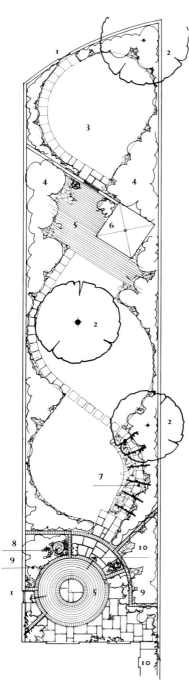

**PLAN FOR A
LONG NARROW GARDEN**

CHANGES IN LEVEL

Once the main linear measurements are complete, check any changes of level. The height of steps and retaining walls is easy enough to note by using a short steel tape measure. Sloping lawns are slightly more difficult, but can be checked by sighting back towards the house so that your eye is level with a particular point and then measuring the distance to the ground.

PREVAILING WINDS

A chill wind can prevent us from enjoying the garden, and for much of the year this will come from a particular 'prevailing' direction. If wind is a problem, check the prevailing direction and mark it on your survey so that you can provide an effective windbreak.

GOOD OR BAD VIEWS

We are so often preoccupied with what goes on within our plot that we tend to forget that there is a world outside. Good views are a bonus and should be left open or even emphasized. Bad views – an overlooking upstairs window or the back of a neighbour's garage – should be screened, either with a solid structure of some kind or by planting.

SOIL

The type of soil in your garden will largely determine what you can grow. Acid soil is at one end of the spectrum and alkaline at the other; plants happy in one type may be quite the opposite in the other. A soil mid-way between the two is neutral and will allow you to grow a wide range of species. Buy a simple soil-testing kit from any garden centre and take samples from various parts of the plot. Most kits provide lists of plants that will thrive in any given soil type.

ASPECT

I have left the most important piece of survey information to last. This involves checking the way the garden faces in relation to the passage of the sun. Checking this is where that compass comes in handy, so you can easily verify the position of north and south. Remember that the sun rises in the east and sets in the west and that in winter it will be a good deal lower and cast longer shadows than in the summer.

Far left: *Courtyards can make fine sheltered gardens which have the benefit of direct access from the house on a number of sides. An architectural design like this one is often the best choice. Setts, that could have been part of the old floor, make ideal paving while the solid roof-supports act as host to scrambling climbers that frame the shady porch.*

Left: *Roof gardens are in a world of their own and, while the views may be superb, the growing conditions can be harsh. Shelter is often vital and this lattice screen is perfect for both plants and people, picking up the pattern of the wrought-iron furniture.*

SQUARE GARDEN

Square gardens are the most difficult of all to design as they are absolutely static. There are two basic ways to handle the problem: either use a circular pattern that will disguise the shape or use a series of interlocking rectangles that build upon the basic outline and create far greater interest from it. This is precisely what I have done in this tiny town garden (left) with a collage of water, paving and planting. Some of the beds are raised to give young planting a boost and to soften the walls, while the overhead beams cast light shade on the sitting area below. The seat and barbecue are built-in to save space in such a limited area and pots of plants, ideal on a terrace or patio, provide instant colour.

PLAN FOR A SQUARE GARDEN

KEY: 1 Raised Bed; 2 Overhead Beams and Climbers; 3 Built-in Seating; 4 Seat; 5 Slatted Fence; 6 York Stone; 7 Brick Paving; 8 Barbecue; 9 Pond; 10 Tree; 11 Mixed Planting; 12 Pots.

Right: *Dividing a garden into separate rooms or areas is an important aspect of garden design. The white bench here nestles into a niche in the hedges, but the eye is drawn into another space by the carefully positioned tree and topiary. The hedges have also been clipped at different heights, with rounded contours that are altogether softer and more comfortable than a crisp rectangular outline. This composition is all about asymmetry: the vertical line and size of the tree act as a counter-balance to the longer and lower line of the hedge below, while the seat acts as a punctuation mark to 'lift' the quiet background.*

Far right: *Why do people always paint picket fences white? White paint can often glare and is a chore to maintain. With a spectrum of colour available, think positive and go for something like this striking blue. You could use the colour somewhere else in the garden – on the weatherboarding of the house or on a well-painted building.*

THE DESIGN

Now that the survey is complete you can start to think about the actual design and just what you want to see in the finished garden. This really is a family job: after all, the finished composition is going to have to cater for everyone and everything. Start to make a list, jotting down every requirement you and other members of your family can think of. In a typical garden this might include a patio for sitting and dining, a barbecue, raised beds, a pool, a lawn and a play area, as well as a shed, a greenhouse, somewhere to put the bikes and an arbour or area of built-in seating. Remember, too, that a garden has to contain the ugly as well as the practical, so the dustbins, washing line, compost heap and incinerator will have to fit somewhere!

If the list seems endless, don't worry – you can always thin it down later. It is more important that you leave nothing out, as it's much more difficult to incorporate a major feature once the design of the garden is complete.

PREPARING A DRAWING

Making a scaled drawing from your survey is straightforward. You will need to use a sheet of graph paper, selecting one or a number of squares to represent a metre or foot on the ground. Starting with the house, transfer all your measurements on to the graph paper, including the position of doors and windows, drains, slopes and everything else you noted down. Mark in the direction of the prevailing wind if there was one, any good or bad views, the length of the shadows and so on. Pretty soon you will have a survey drawing, which will provide the basis for the finished design. Take several photocopies and file the original drawing for safe-keeping.

To prepare the final design drawing, stick a copy of the survey on to a clean surface and fix a sheet of tracing paper over it. At first, just rough in the broad position of features. The area allocated for a patio might logically be at the rear of the house if it is in full sun, but if shade is a problem it may be some distance away, served by a sensible path. A barbecue would ideally be close to the kitchen, a pond in full view of the main windows of the house, while the shed, greenhouse and utility areas should be grouped together, and screened in some way. If your plans include an arbour, this could be sited in a quiet corner. Work in pencil and have an eraser handy to rub out any mistakes. You can also sketch in alternatives before making a final choice: there are bound to be plenty of changes initially!

At this stage, just allocate space so that the garden starts to work in overall terms. You needn't worry about exact dimensions of a feature or the pattern and material for the paving until slightly later on.

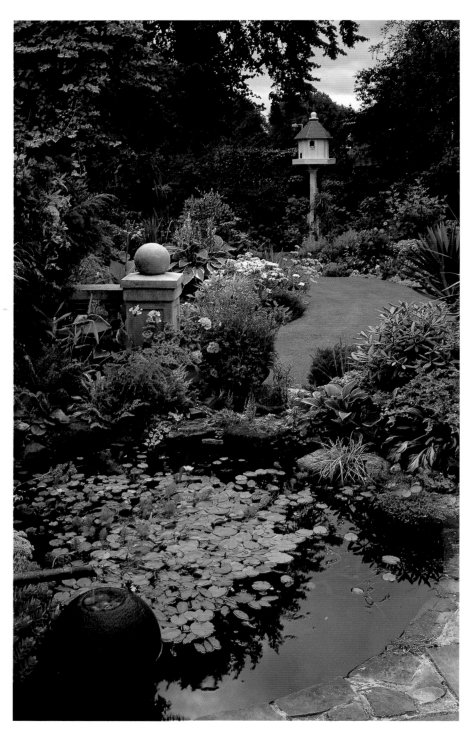

HARD LANDSCAPING

Once you are happy with the approximate position and the size of each feature, you can fill in the detail by firming the design up and finalizing the list of features you want to incorporate. It's worth bearing in mind that the 'hard landscape' areas of paving and walling will take the lion's share of any budget. Plan these to link sensibly with the adjoining house. If the building is of brick, then brick might also be used in part of the patio or to build raised beds; if the floors inside the building are stone then this could be run outside to form a patio that will link the two elements together.

As has already been emphasized, simplicity is so often the key to success. By keeping the materials used for hard surfaces to a minimum, you are far more likely to achieve a harmonious result. Of course, a large expanse of garden covered in a single material may look visually heavy – especially if you are using new bricks or concrete paviors – and in such instances it can be a positive benefit to mix materials: a brick path flanked by stone setts or railway sleepers, or a chequerboard pattern of flagstones and cobbles. Never underestimate, either, the softening effects of sympathetic planting: shrubs spilling over on to a path, or grass and moss growing in the cracks between bricks or paviors can do wonders to mellow even the most recently landscaped plot, integrating your hard surfaces with the garden to create a living outdoor room.

More 'fluid' surfacing materials include gravel, cobbles and even tarmac. These can be laid to a flowing pattern, and are ideal for a sweeping driveway or a meandering path, where granite setts or flagstones would need to be cut to fit. They can also demand less on the eye than other, larger-module materials, something to be borne in mind, particularly in smaller gardens.

If you look at the designs in this chapter you will also see that the layout close to the house is planned in an 'architectural' and positive way, helping to draw house and garden together as a single entity. Further away you can start to think in more fluid terms, planning the shape of lawns and borders in strong flowing curves. These provide a real feeling of room and movement, which in turn creates an impression of greater space, even in a compact garden.

PLAN FOR A TRIANGULAR
GARDEN

PLANTING

While the planting scheme is beyond the scope of
this book, it is, of course, the essential element
that brings any garden to life, the plants
embracing your composition so that they clothe
and soften the inevitably hard lines of paving and
walling. I think I have already made it clear that
trying to create a garden without planning it first
will almost certainly lead to disaster. This is
particularly true of planting. At all costs, avoid
over-complicated planting schemes. Do your
homework, check a good plant directory, and go
about this all-important planning in a logical
sequence – it will pay enormous dividends in the
long run. Think first about where you might
position trees, bearing in mind their size and
their ability to provide shade or a screen. Next
plan your shrubs: fast-growing evergreens will
quickly provide shelter and protection. Finally,
fill in the details and add colour with a selection
of bulbs and herbaceous perennials, and set aside
areas for annuals and containers for a change of
planting from year to year.

TRIANGULAR GARDEN

Triangular gardens are always awkward as they
tend to focus the view in a particular direction.
In this design I have demonstrated the principle
of providing an architectural pattern close to the
building. The brick paving leads out from the
French windows and interlocks with the raised
bed and planting to form an attractive
combination of hard and soft landscape. From
here the eye is led away at an angle, under the
pergola and towards the raised pool.

The apex of the triangle is naturally dominant
and virtually impossible to hide. It is best not to
bother; soften it by all means with well-chosen
plants, but allow the eye to rest there with a
purpose. The seat, placed alongside a tree at the
end of this garden, has the added bonus of an
attractive view back across the garden.

KEY: 1 Tree; 2 Seat on Brick Paving; 3 Mixed
Planting; 4 Raised Pool and Spout; 5 Wall; 6 Pots;
7 Pergola; 8 Herbs; 9 Stepping Stones; 10 Raised
Bed for Annuals; 11 Roses; 12 Brick Paving.

Opposite: *Water is a delightful
influence in any garden, but needs
to match the mood of the overall
design. In this situation, the
informal pool echoes the sweep of
lawn that is in turn softened by
planting. While a calm surface sets
up reflections, a little movement
adds enormous interest. The flume
in the foreground is designed to
allow a trickle of water to
overflow the bowl and drop into
the pool below. A dovecot
provides a more distant focal
point against trees and shrubs.*

Above left: *This window through
a garden wall focuses the view
beyond to glorious effect. A
glimpse provides that vital
element of mystery as well as
creating a feeling of tension
before you enter the next 'room'.*

PATHS
AND PATIOS

*Paths and patios are the hard landscape 'bones' of your garden
and provide the design framework around which the
softer elements of lawns, planting and other features can be
positioned. They are crucial to your enjoyment of the
garden, providing areas for sitting, dining, play and many other
activities as well as access to other features.
Simplicity and strength of purpose are all-important in this part
of the design. You should choose your materials carefully
from the vast range available, taking your time over the choice
and thinking about the visual and cost implications.
Paving is perhaps the most long-term investment in your
garden; make sure it is right for you and your situation before
you buy. Any paving close to the house will relate
strongly to it, so this should also influence your choice. Look
around your area to see what materials predominate
locally, and use them for the most sympathetic result.*

*All the materials used here are
natural rather than man-made,
which allows them to relate to
one another. The gravel path
provides a purpose for the old
wire pergola and the paving gives
a place to sit, while the planting
draws the composition together.
The bowls, piled high with flints,
provide a humorous counterpoint.*

Left: This path is built from granite setts, with a step constructed from the same material. Planting softens the outline to either side, and moss has been allowed to grow up in the gaps between the setts. The stone spheres provide attractive and unusual punctuation.

Opposite: Gravel is an ideal surface for a circular patio as it will take up any shape. This design is built up from a series of circles that include the outer ring of planting, the brick-edged pool, the terracotta pots and even the stone orbs. The gentle curves naturally incline the eye to the pond, which acts as a focal point. Only the sundial and the seat disrupt the pattern.

Apart from the aesthetics of choosing the right material for a patio or path, you will also need to allocate enough space, particularly for a patio. If you think of your garden as an outside room, or series of rooms, then the main paved terrace will take up a similar proportion of the available area to, say, your sitting-room inside the house. An absolute minimum size would be 3.6 × 3.6m (12 × 12ft) which provides enough space for four people to sit around a table. If you can make it more generous, then do so: far better to be able to push a chair back with plenty of room to spare than risk tipping over into the nearest flower bed with a drink in your hand!

The overall shape of the paving will be important too. This is often the first point of entry into the garden, especially at the front of the house and is likely to set the theme for the entire composition. There may be scope here for raised beds, and in the back garden for built-in seating and a barbecue. Overhead beams can provide light shade and are invaluable in screening you from an adjacent window. Train a climber over them to soften the line and provide fragrance for the area below. If high walls flank your patio, they can also support climbers or may be used to extend a colour scheme from inside to

out. This is particularly effective in a town garden linked to the house by floor-to-ceiling windows or sliding patio doors. Water is another option, ranging from the formality of a rectangular pool, complete with fountain, to a simple millstone, set within an area of loose cobbles and planting, with water sliding over the surface from a tank concealed below.

While patios concentrate activity in a given area, paths are built for access, both around the house and through the garden. The smoother the surface, the quicker the action: a crisp surface of precast slabs encourages speed, while a path laid with irregular cobbles slows you down, both visually and physically. Very often the material chosen for the patio will be suitable for the paths too, providing continuity. But whatever you use, do make sure the path is wide enough, remembering that it may well have planting to either side that will spill over and soften the outline, reducing the width to some extent.

Whatever your final choice, remember that the materials for a patio or path will last a lifetime. They form the basic framework of your garden, and can only be changed with difficulty and at great expense, in terms of time, money and inconvenience. Planning is therefore vital.

BRICK

Brick paving is extremely versatile. If your house is also built of brick, you can use it in the garden to create strong visual links between the two areas. It can be teamed with another surface if used as panels or contrasting courses, or laid alone to make a superb path or patio. Because a brick is a small module it can be laid to a curving or circular pattern without cutting, making it particularly suitable for the sweeping line of a path or for a strongly shaped patio.

Before buying bricks you should always check the density. A rough meaure of this can be made by twisting a coin on the surface as hard as possible. If no damage is apparent then the surface will be pretty resistant. Not all bricks are suitable for paving. Only the harder types will withstand the pressures of feet and frost. Up until a few years ago the choice was between house-facing bricks or very hard and shiny 'engineering' bricks. While these can still be used – and engineering bricks look very good in a crisp 'architectural' situation – purpose-made brick 'paviors' that are about half the thickness of a standard house brick are now produced in a variety of styles.

Brick paving should be laid over a sub-base of well-compacted hardcore and either bedded on a semi-dry mortar mix, with dry mortar brushed into the joints, or on a wet mortar mix, with careful pointing of the joints to avoid any staining of the surface. Another method uses bricks butted together, without mortar, over a layer of hardcore. The edges of a path or patio must be firmly set in concrete to prevent movement of the overall surface.

A number of different 'bonds' (patterns) can be used, each of which has a different visual emphasis. Stretcher bond along a path tends to accelerate a view, but if laid in the opposite direction, across the path, it slows the eye down. Herringbone is a complicated and relatively 'busy' pattern, while basketweave bond is altogether more static.

Because of their textured surface, bricks soon mellow and can be quickly colonized by mosses and lichens. This makes them ideal in a traditional design or a cottage garden where the patina of age looks just right.

Herringbone is a visually complicated but fascinating pattern that is often used in a traditional design situation. Here the surface is delightfully covered with mosses and lichens, adding to the feeling of age and maturity.

Opposite above left: This crisply designed path is made of bricks butted together in a basketweave pattern without mortar joints. The soldier-course edging is softened by overhanging plants.

Opposite above right: This path illustrates the way that bricks can be laid to a curving pattern. Stretcher bond leads the eye on to the timber bridge, although the step here is perhaps too shallow, making a trip likely.

Opposite below left: These old bricks look just right laid dry in a basketweave pattern. The unpointed, irregular bonds offer the chance to introduce low-growing plants such as thyme. The planting ensures that this is a path for a stroll rather than a brisk walk, while the perfectly positioned copper pot provides a pleasing focal point.

Opposite below right: A brick floor is ideal for use in courtyard gardens. This carefully laid herringbone-pattern patio provides plenty of room for sitting and entertaining. The plant-filled terracotta pots add a pretty splash of colour, while the lush surrounding foliage softens the garden walls.

Right: *A gravel path is attractive, practical and associates particularly well with planting. And the crunch of gravel under-foot has a particular charisma all its own. This path is neatly edged with boards and passes beneath a well-detailed pergola.*

Below: *This Japanese-style path simulates the bed of a stream, with rocks and boulders breaking the flow. The thin, sculptural leaves of iris are the perfect foil to the water-washed stones.*

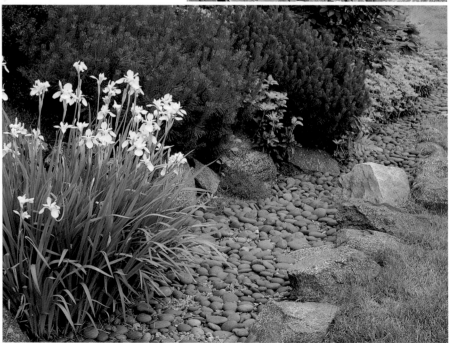

GRAVEL

Gravel is a versatile, attractive and relatively cheap paving material. It can look equally at home as the base for a patio in a formal town garden or as a sweeping drive in the country, but correct laying is essential if you are to avoid an uncomfortable 'treadmill' effect when trying to cross your path or patio.

Always ensure that gravel is laid on a solid sub-base of well-compacted hardcore, the thickness of which should be between 7cm (3in) and 15cm (6in), depending on the underlying soil type and the amount of traffic – either cars or pedestrians. Over the hardcore lay a 5cm (2in) layer of 5cm (2in) diameter gravel and roll this well in. The next layer will be a 5cm (2in) layer of fine gravel, mixed with hoggin – a clay mixture available from the same gravel pit. This will act as a binder to the final layer of 1cm ($\frac{3}{8}$in) diameter washed pea gravel that should be top-dressed over the surface and rolled well in. To ensure the final finish is well compacted and firm underfoot, a heavy roller should be used over the surface at all stages of the job.

Unlike paving, gravel is a 'fluid' surface and often needs retaining at the edges. One option is to use long timber boards or railway sleepers, treated with non-toxic preservative and pegged in position with stakes. A more handsome, and more expensive, alternative would be to use bricks set in concrete. Precast concrete kerb edging should be avoided, particularly if curved borders are required.

Where gravel adjoins planting, it can be simply run under the latter without a defining edge so that the two surfaces overlap one another. Plants can also be spot-planted within an area of gravel and broad foliage acts as an excellent foil to the much smaller stones. If, however, you use gravel next to grass, you should ensure the grass is set at least 10cm (4in) above the gravel surface and is retained at the edges. This will prevent stones from being caught in mower blades when you cut the grass. Maintenance is generally low, although fallen leaves can be a nuisance, requiring regular raking in the autumn.

Gravel is available in a wide variety of colours, depending on its area of origin. Pale gravel has a great ability to reflect light, and you can use this to good advantage in shady areas or basement gardens. White chippings will transform a gloomy corner, looking particularly effective when teamed with another contrasting surface such as slate. Another point in gravel's favour is its use as a burglar deterrent or guest early-warning system, since it's impossible to approach a house along a gravel path or drive without immediately alerting the residents. However, parents of small children may have less positive feelings about gravel. There is no doubt that children find it hard on the knees when they fall, and they do tend to enjoy 'sowing' it all over the lawn, giving their parents the less enjoyable task of sweeping it off again. There is also the danger that children will put the gravel in their mouths, which is unhygienic and could be dangerous.

CHIPPINGS

While gravel is normally rounded, stone chippings are usually angular. Smaller than cobbles, chippings, like gravel, come in a variety of colours. Often the main hard surfacing material in formal Japanese gardens, chippings can be used to dramatic effect. In a basement town garden, a hard surface area covered in white chippings (obtained from calcinated flint stone) will help to maximize the available light, reflecting it and 'opening up' the space. And plants with dark green foliage look particularly striking growing alongside white chippings. Wood and bark chippings, although more commonly used as a ground mulch to help prevent weeds, can look effective as surfaces for pathways in rural environments and lend gardens an organic feel.

The different textures of gravels, glass marbles and ceramics are contrasted in this delightful garden by Hilary McMahon. Broad steps drop down to a pool, with a gravel beach that is in turn flanked by planting. The maintenance requirements of this garden are extremely low.

STONE

NATURAL STONE

This is the most expensive and finest paving available. It can be found in a vast range of types, colours, shapes and textures, looking superb in any well-designed garden.

As with all surfaces, it should be used within the overall context of the setting. While fine, old, second-hand sandstone flags would naturally look out of place adjoining a high-tech steel-and-glass façade, the same stone would look superb laid as a terrace in a more traditional situation. Random rectangular slabs of stone of uneven thickness are often available, and can be laid on carefully levelled and compacted ground with a bed of sifted soil or sand. This type of paving need not necessarily be pointed, and joints can be left open to allow colonization by low, ground-hugging plants. You should work out a paving pattern from a central 'key' stone and try to ensure that the joints between the slabs are staggered. Small spaces can be left empty to form planting pockets or filled with brick to relieve the appearance.

SLATE

In contrast to natural stone, slate has a naturally sleek, architectural appearance and often looks better wet than dry. Its dark colour ideally suits it to a sunny situation, where it can either form an entire terrace or path, or be used in strips or squares to contrast with another kind of paving.

GRANITE

Every bit as hard as it looks, granite is often hewn into brick-sized full setts or smaller half setts. The surface is slightly uneven, so it is not always ideal for a patio where tables and chairs are present, but setts are ideal for a path or drive, where the surface offers greater grip than a smooth paving.

MARBLE

The exorbitant cost of marble is usually enough to deter most people from using it to lay a patio. It is undeniably exotic and, while it looks great in an Italian piazza, it looks appalling used as crazy paving in a suburban garden. Just occasionally it fits into a highly controlled pattern adjoining a contemporary building, but it should usually be avoided.

Granite setts are easily laid to a pattern. This fan shape is both traditional and attractive. The somewhat harsh colour is tempered by grass, while the irregularity of the stones emphasizes the natural character of the material.

Opposite above left: Stepping stones draw both the eye and foot across a lawn or planted area. This path meanders towards a distant arch and disappears, with a slight air of mystery, before finally reaching the house.

Opposite above right: These slate slabs are butted tightly together, at an angle to the surrounding bricks, to form a perfectly smooth and sophisticated patio. The planting has been particularly well chosen and positioned to temper the crisp composition.

Opposite below: Solid riven slabs of stone form a stepping-stone path through a bed of loose cobbles. Simple timber boards contain the cobbles, while a predominantly green planting scheme provides a quiet background.

TIMBER

Timber is ideal for many projects in the garden, and is particularly useful for decking and steps. Like a stone patio adjacent to a stone house, a wooden deck adjoining a timber building will make a strong link between inside and outside. Timber can be easily worked to shapes that would be extremely difficult to produce using paving. It is light, it warms up quickly and it needs little maintenance apart from a regular application of non-toxic preservative. Never use creosote, which is certain death to plants. Some wood can even be bought already pressure-treated with preservative, further reducing after-care. Remember, though, that timber means trees, and if those trees come from a non-managed source then you are contributing to the degradation of our environment. Please check with your supplier, particularly if you envisage using hardwood species from tropical rain forests.

The sturdy and heavy bulk of railway sleepers makes them ideal for paving, raised beds and retaining walls. Try and select your sleepers before you buy, as they may be soaked with oil or tar which will cause you problems in hot weather. Because of their weight, it really is a two-man job to lift them, but they are solid enough to be bedded on a minimal foundation of sifted soil over well-compacted ground or they can be laid in a staggered bond like brickwork. Raised beds are fast to build, and again the sleepers can be laid like bricks, their weight allowing them to be laid dry. However, if you are constructing a retaining wall, or a raised bed that is more than three sleepers high, the timbers should be drilled to accept vertical steel rods that are then bedded into a concrete foundation to ensure stability.

If your garden includes a change in level, sleepers can make excellent steps. Rather than making a straight flight, you might prefer a staggered pattern with planting encroaching on either side. Steps can also be built from logs, securely pegged into the slope. In a steep flight they should be bedded close together, but with a more gentle gradient the treads can be floored with chipped bark.

Raised beds or retaining walls can be built from sawn logs arranged vertically to follow any line, straight or curved. Assuming the logs will rise about 600mm (24in) above ground, you should bury them 300mm (12in) below ground for stability, first soaking them thoroughly in a non-toxic preservative.

Large logs can be sliced up into discs about 15cm (6in) thick and used as stepping stones. More unusually, they could even be made to form a kind of patio. If they become slippery, chicken wire nailed over each slice will solve the problem and be virtually invisible.

Above: Logs set into a slope and firmly pegged in place make a delightfully informal flight of steps. Such a feature invites you to explore the garden and creates a practical and interesting focal point. Here the treads are left simply as rougher grass with planting softening the edges, but chipped bark or gravel could be used instead.

Opposite: Timber has been used at all levels in this garden. The deck is built from neatly squared boards and the theme is continued in the well-detailed raised beds. At the highest level the overhead beams would provide excellent supports for climbing plants and will cast light shade, extending the line of the patio out into the surrounding planting.

DECKING

This deck measures about 3.6m (12ft) square and provides an informal seating area, close to a large pool. The boards have been carefully 'distressed' to expose the grain. This was achieved by lightly burning the surface of the wood with a blow lamp and then using a wire brush to remove the softer parts of the timber, leaving the tougher grain slightly raised.

CONSTRUCTION

Mark out the area to be covered by the deck and remove any turf. Next, excavate to a depth of 100–150mm (4–6in), then backfill the area with crushed stone or gravel. Make sure this is well compacted and that the surface is level.

The height of the deck should be 150–300mm (6–12in). The deck shown here is supported on joists that run between 100 × 100mm (4 × 4in) posts protruding 300mm (12in) above the ground. Cut the posts to length: you will need to sink them about 450mm (18in) into the ground, and then allow for the 300mm (12in) height plus an additional 50mm (2in) that projects above the supporting joists. Soak all the timber in a non-toxic, exterior-grade wood preservative and leave to dry.

SETTING OUT THE POSTS

Datum post

BOLTING THE JOISTS IN PLACE

6mm plywood spacer

FIXING THE DECK BOARDS

Calculate the positions of the second row of posts by using one of the $150 \times 50mm$ $(6 \times 2in)$ joists marked up with the post spacings as a template. Set up a line at right angles to the datum post and accurately set the corner post. Check the post is vertical and the top is level with the datum post by using a spirit level and straight edge from the opposite post on the first side. Repeat for the remaining posts, and ram or concrete in place.

Using 'G' cramps, cramp a joist along the inside of one pair of posts, 50mm (2in) down from the top of the posts plus the thickness of the deck boards. Mark the top and bottom of the joist on all posts and extend these lines to the sides using a square. Mark bolt hole positions on the posts diagonally within the rectangles and drill clearance holes just large enough for the bolts.

Cramp a joist between a pair of posts so that it extends 50mm (2in) each end. Use the clearance holes in the post as a template to drill through the joist. Repeat for a second joist on the opposite side of the posts. Counterbore one of the joists to accept the nuts, then bolt both joists to the posts using 200mm (8in) long M12 ($\frac{1}{2}$in) carriage bolts. Repeat for all joists.

To fit the deck, position the first board 6mm ($\frac{1}{4}$in) clear of the line of posts by using plywood spacers and screw down into the centre of each joist. Use the spacers to position the second board. Screw in place. Continue across the deck.

You can build a step leading up to the deck by setting three posts outside the decking but opposite and parallel to three of the main posts. Bolt $75 \times 50mm$ ($3 \times 2in$) bearers between them and the corresponding main deck posts, directly beneath the joists. The central post is cut short to fit under a step at deck level. Cut the outer posts about 900mm (36in) longer for the handrail, which is recessed to the inside faces of the posts. Glue and screw in place.

Bore or dig a hole 550mm (22in) deep using a post-hole borer or a spade. Fill the bottom of the hole with 100mm (4in) of well-rammed hardcore and set the post top to a level 50mm (2in) above the proposed deck surface. This will be the 'datum' post. All the other posts are set out from this and checked against it. Check the post for vertical in both directions using a spirit level and then ram soil around the post or set it in concrete to hold it in place. If you use concrete, bring the mix slightly higher than ground level and round it over so that water runs away from the post. Leave the concrete to dry.

Mark out the remaining five post positions down one side of the deck at 680mm (27in) centres. Bore the remaining holes and position the posts as described above. Make sure that the tops of all the posts are level: use a straight edge and spirit level to check this, always working from the datum post.

Now work out the distance to the opposite side. I suggest using a random arrangement of $150 \times 25mm$ ($6 \times 1in$) and $175 \times 25mm$ ($7 \times 1in$) boards which will have been planed down by about 6mm ($\frac{1}{4}$in). Allow for a 6mm ($\frac{1}{4}$in) gap between each board to assist drainage.

OPTIONAL STEP

Above: *Where space is limited, the only option is to build upwards. This is a pedestal for pots on a three-tier wooden platform. Plant colour is mainly restricted to greys and pinks, teaming perfectly with the soft tones of terracotta.*

Right: *Breakfast on a warm patio is a pleasure no one should deny themselves, but remember that garden furnishings should blend well with their environment. These wickerwork seats have been chosen to echo the warm colour of the stone sets.*

Opposite above: *This roof garden is floored with lightweight tiles and surrounded by raised beds. White-painted screens help to filter the wind, while the pots are safely positioned away from the parapet walls.*

Opposite below: *Pots of plants will soften the flat expanse of a large patio, providing instant colour throughout the year. Here, the uniform colour of the terracotta pots provides visual continuity.*

PATIOS

A patio is very often the hub of activity around which the rest of the garden revolves. In some cases, such as a courtyard or tiny town garden, it can take up almost the entire area available, with planting softening the edges of the plot. In a larger composition it may share the space with sweeping lawns, borders, raised beds, vegetable plots and a range of other features.

As well as providing a site for sitting and dining, most patios have to cater for children's play, household chores and the repair of anything from bikes to car engines. We have already seen that you need ample space and have looked at the wide range of materials available for construction. If in doubt, and you can afford it, always make the patio larger than you initially think; it will be well worth it later on.

Of course the area may not always be at ground level: roof gardens are immensely attractive, even though they do pose all kinds of problems in constructional and horticultural terms. It is exciting to create an outside room in this Mary Poppins world of wide skies and chimney pots, but always check that the roof is strong enough to take the additional weight required. If in doubt, call on the services of a qualified architect or surveyor. His or her fee will be more than worth it if you are then able to rest easy at night without the horrific prospect of a ton of soggy compost arriving unexpectedly on your bed! Other aspects of safety are also important: a pot knocked over at ground level is no problem, but the same container falling from a roof could be very dangerous indeed.

Because a patio is essentially a hard landscape feature it will benefit enormously from the provision of planting. As a general rule plants grow far better in the ground than in pots. So, although pots are invaluable for instant colour throughout the year, you should try to leave some areas in and around your patio open for plants. Raised beds are both practical and attractive options for the patio: you can vary the soil in them to suit a particular type of planting, you can use their sides as occasional seating, and if you wish to provide an area for children, you can convert them to sandpits or other play areas which can later revert to their original purpose.

Opposite above: *This outside room has been as carefully designed as any within the house. The circular pattern of setts has been beautifully laid in concentric courses, the round table sitting right in the middle. The table cloth and chair covers match this pattern, while following the pink, blue and mauve colours of the attractive planting scheme.*

Opposite below: *Who said romance was dead? What could be more charming than sitting in this idyllic setting beneath the trees, sharing dinner? The rest of the garden and world are incidental, it's the moment that counts.*

Above: *Dining in such a pretty gazebo is definitely up-market, but nevertheless delightful. On a practical note, the roof provides shelter in case of rain.*

Above right: *Tea on the terrace is a perfect way to spend a summer afternoon. Wicker furniture always looks good in a garden and is light enough to move around easily. Gravel provides a sensible floor, allowing planting to grow through the surface.*

Right: *Some barbecues are gas-fired, either from a bottle stored below or from a piped mains supply. This one is of ample size, with plenty of room on the terrace to allow unhindered cooking; planting at the side would greatly soften the impact and blend the barbecue into the overall composition.*

OUTDOOR EATING

One of the best reasons for having a patio of ample size is that it allows you to take meals outside. To do this comfortably you need a dining area that is well sheltered, both from cold winds and any overlooking windows that threaten privacy. Because paving and walling are likely to predominate, planting will be essential. It is worth remembering that this often provides a much more effective filter for the wind than a solid fence or screen.

Fragrance is another benefit of carefully chosen planting in this area, especially if you train climbers along overhead beams. There is nothing more delightful than sitting outside surrounded by such plants as honeysuckle, jasmine or roses. Many species are at their most scented in the evening, at just the time when you are likely to use the patio most.

Subtle lighting is essential if you are going to get the best out of your outside room. As well as the straightforward illumination of an area in practical terms, you have the option of highlighting a particular feature or focal point. But, as with any aspect of design, keep things as simple as possible. There are some ghastly fittings available that are not only pretentious but downright ugly. Remember that it is the light that is important, not the fitting. The location of a beam or soft glow is also important: there is little point in illuminating the top of your head, but a fitting positioned at working height beside a barbecue or at ground level close to steps can be practical as well as attractive.

Lighting requires electricity, and one option is to install a completely waterproof ring main around your garden. This can be used to power various tools and features, but you should always bear safety in mind, and it is strongly recommended that you take professional advice and enrol the services of a fully qualified electrician if in any doubt whatsoever.

Finally, don't forget that we're not the only creatures to eat outside – birds, mammals and a multitude of insects live out there too. A bird table or bath is an essential garden feature, and if you can avoid the use of pesticides and sprays then make every effort to do so, as it will benefit the flora and fauna.

BARBECUE

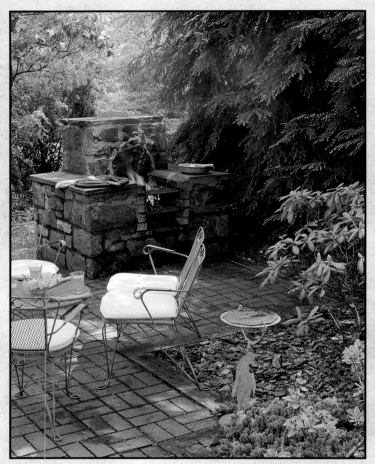

Eating outside is one of the great pleasures in life but if you like barbecuing, and millions do, then you should go about it in a positive way. Small, 'off-the-peg' affairs can rarely cook enough for a gathering of ravenous friends: what you need is a stout, well-built, purpose-made job of the kind shown here.

It is simplest to plan such a feature in the initial stages of building a patio but, if you are careful, you could incorporate it into an existing layout, as long as solid foundations are dug.

Protect your patio while building by covering the surrounding surface with heavy-gauge polythene, lapping the edges of the sheets into the excavation and weighting them down.

BACK ELEVATION

SIDE ELEVATION

FRONT ELEVATION

CONSTRUCTION

Excavate a 200mm (8in) deep rectangular base measuring 2 × 1.5m (6ft 6in × 4ft 6in). Spread an even layer of hardcore in the bottom of the excavation and compact this to a finished thickness of 100mm (4in). Spread sharp sand across the surface to fill in any gaps. Cover the hardcore with 100mm (4in) of *concrete and level this off flush with the surrounding surface using a straight-edged board. Leave the concrete to dry for a week; to ensure that it dries evenly, keep it covered with damp sacks if the weather is hot, and with polythene or sheeting of some other kind if there is a chance of frost.*

Plan the stonework in advance by laying the pattern out on the ground. The barbecue shown here has a worktop height of about 800mm (31in) and a height to the top of the flue of 1295mm (51in). Avoid vertical joints in succeeding courses (layers) that coincide with one another. At the corners, blocks should be bonded together so that they overlap and provide greater strength. You can draw the plan and elevations out on tracing paper, but take several copies as some will be bound to get dirty or lost! The sizes we have used are: 190×65mm ($7\frac{1}{2} \times 2\frac{1}{2}$in); 215×65mm ($8\frac{1}{2} \times 2\frac{1}{2}$in); 290×65mm ($11\frac{1}{2} \times 2\frac{1}{2}$in); 290×137mm ($11\frac{1}{2} \times 5\frac{1}{2}$in); 290×215mm ($11\frac{1}{2} \times 8\frac{1}{2}$in); and 445×65mm ($17\frac{1}{2} \times 2\frac{1}{2}$in); all of the blocks are 100mm (4in) thick. The barbecue also needs 50mm (2in) thick copings measuring 610×260mm ($24 \times 10\frac{1}{4}$in) and 610×125mm (24×5in), and 610×610mm (24×24in) paving slabs.

First construct the four supporting walls to a height of 225mm (9in).

Bed the slabs beneath the charcoal tray between the two centre supporting walls; one course higher, bed the floor slabs for the log store on the right-hand side. Lay a course of coping on top of the slabs, then build up the centre walls, inserting 100×6mm ($4 \times \frac{1}{4}$in) mild steel strips, 1220mm (48in) long, to support the charcoal tray and the cooking grid as indicated. Bed angled copings above the fifth course of bricks to give a neat finish. Build up the front, back and two end walls to the height of the centre supporting walls, incorporating a coping course at the back to maintain the correct bonding. Openings in the back wall provide additional useful storage space.

PREPARING THE BASE

Hardcore

Concrete

Patio

Back

Concrete

Hardcore

THE SUPPORTING WALLS

Two paving slabs each side are used to form the worktops. The flue arch is supported by a semi-circular 'turning piece' with an internal radius of 290mm ($11\frac{1}{2}$in). It is made from a 1220mm (48in) length of 100×6mm ($4 \times \frac{1}{4}$in) mild steel strip bent into shape: the ends should be bent at right angles to form 100mm (4in) projections. Make up a plywood template and take that to a blacksmith or steel fabricator who can make the turning piece for you.

Bed the turning piece in mortar. Build up the blocks for the flue section around the arch, one course at a time. A number of blocks will need cutting to fit around the arch, using a hammer and bolster. Carefully score all around the block where you want the break to be. Bed the block in sand, then give one or two sharp blows with a hammer and bolster to sever the block. Careful pointing will make up any discrepancies in the cutting.

Leave a gap of approximately 300×150mm (12×6in) at the top of the back wall, below which is a loose, angled coping block. This can be adjusted to achieve a good draught through the flue. Finally, cap the flue with one or more continuous lengths of slab.

FLUE DETAIL

Top

Back

Flue

FORMING THE WORKTOPS

STEEL STRIPS FOR TRAY AND GRILL

ARCH SUPPORT DETAIL

SEATING SENSE

One of my prime rules of garden design is that you should never be a slave to your valuable outside room. If you are a keen gardener, prepared to spend plenty of time on cultivation and maintenance, then that's fine. If you are not, a carefully designed composition will ensure you never have to spend more than a minimal amount of time looking after the space. But whether you are a keen gardener or a lazy one, sitting outside on a hot summer's day is one of life's great, simple pleasures. The choice of furniture is extensive, ranging from custom-made built-in designs to an almost unlimited variety of off-the-peg tables and chairs. The main consideration is that your choice reflects the underlying theme of the garden as a whole. While well-conceived moulded plastic chairs in primary colours can be great to sit in and look perfect in a modern design, they will appear quite awful in a period setting. In other words, think and look carefully before you buy or build, and if you are buying furniture always try it out. It's surprising how often a really elegant-looking chair can be appallingly uncomfortable.

Fine trees are often a focal point in a garden. A seat built around a tree will be visually attractive and will also benefit from the cool shade of a broad canopy of leaves.

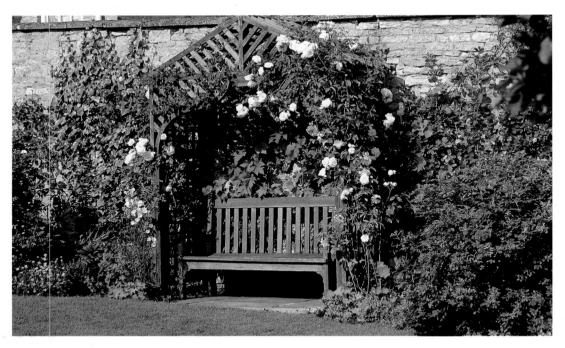

While it is outside the abilities of the average home craftsman to build elaborate seating in metal or plastics, most projects that involve timber are well within reach, particularly if you take your time and carefully work out a sensible design beforehand.

Other objects and features in a garden often become occasional seats, and it may be worth taking this into account when choosing them. For example, the edge of a raised bed or pool approximately 45cm (18in) off the ground is at a perfect height for perching, but if it's only one brick thick it won't be that comfortable. A double-brick wall, or one with a rounded brick coping or paving-slab top, will be altogether better. Such a feature will also be part of the overall composition and as such will fit comfortably within the design.

Built-in timber seats can be both practical and attractive. They can be fitted into the angle formed by two house walls, built as an integral part of a barbecue area or form one or more sides of a timber deck. The railway sleepers that we looked at earlier for paving and raised beds (page 26) make ideal seats. Set them on sections of vertical sleeper sunk into the ground, but make

sure they are clean and not smothered with oil, which will make them totally unsuitable for use as seating in hot weather.

In a less formal situation large sections of fallen or felled tree trunks can be fashioned with a chainsaw to make a set of furniture. Chairs can be cut from single sections of timber and the table formed from a number of planks or, if the trunk is big enough, a large diameter slice.

One of the most attractive seating ideas I have seen, and something I am incorporating into my own new garden, uses really large water-worn boulders. These must be substantial, so you will need mechanical means to shift them and partly bury them, but once in a carefully allocated position, close to or even surrounded by paving, they look quite superb. They also look good in an area of gravel and sculptural planting, but do need selecting personally from a stone merchant to get the right shape and character.

As with the other elements of garden design, avoid conflicting styles of furniture, and try to choose designs that are sympathetic to the overall look of your garden. Remember that painted finishes will require frequent retouching if they are not to become shabby.

Right: *A shady sitting area is often essential in a sunny garden, and this woodland retreat fits the bill perfectly. Both the seat and arbour are built from rustic timbers, reflecting the backdrop and canopy of trees. The one element missing is the provision of a fragrant climber – honeysuckle, the traditional woodbine, would be the absolutely perfect choice.*

Right below: *Hammocks have a charm all their own, even if they are the very devil to get in and out of safely. Swinging gently beneath a shady branch is guaranteed to bring on a nap, but do make sure the limb of the tree is completely sound, otherwise you may come down to earth sooner than you had intended!*

Opposite: *This is definitely a set-piece sitting area. But for all that it is both practical and attractive: the brick steps and paving set it apart from the rest of the garden and the crisp outline of the seat stands out in sharp relief against the darker hedge. Planting is essential here to soften the naturally architectural outline, the broad-leaved hostas being a particularly effective touch.*

Just where you sit in the garden is another consideration and, while most patios are sited to catch the sun for much of the day, there is often a real need for a shady corner in which to relax. Such a sitting area can be an altogether smaller and quieter affair, probably positioned away from the house but linked back to it by a path. A backdrop of trees will often be enough to provide shade, but make sure you don't position a seat under a lime with its sticky drip.

Trees will also be the perfect hosts for a hammock, one of the most comfortable places for a quiet snooze. Do make sure the trunks are stout enough, though, and if you suspend the hammock from overhead branches, then check these for any weakness or rot. Hammocks need to be of an ample size – the small ones are simply uncomfortable. They also take a deal of practice to get in and out of, with a few tumbles in the process. Some hammocks come complete with stands, which is fine if you have no trees, but somehow that essential magic is lost.

While much furniture, including hammocks, is essentially static, it can be useful to have a number of light, folding chairs that can be moved around to chase sun or shade as the mood takes you and that can be tucked away in a minimal space for winter storage. Deck chairs were the traditional solution, and I think these still have a great deal of visual appeal. Equally comfortable and attractive are 'director's' folding chairs. The fabric covers of such seats can pick up a colourway used in the house if you will use them indoors as well as out, or provide the basis of a whole exterior colour scheme, taking in awnings over windows, blinds, cushions, paint and even your planting arrangements.

Plastic furniture is reasonably priced and almost maintenance-free. While it can look a little stark, there has recently been a vast improvement in the quality and range of designs available. Again, the sympathetic use of fabrics will enable you to co-ordinate the furniture with your chosen planting scheme.

Exterior bean bags are one of the best new ideas I have seen. They consist of a water-repellent fabric filled with polystyrene granules. The size can be varied, but as a general rule the bigger the better. They are terrific for kids and adults alike and can be used just as well indoors.

TREE SEAT

A tree seat makes a charming focal point in a garden. This octagonal seat sits comfortably around a tree trunk approximately 950mm (36in) in diameter. But you should be able to adapt the measurements to fit the dimensions of your tree. If you build the seat to fit around a relatively young tree, remember to leave room to allow for growth and expansion of the tree trunk. Many garden centres now sell quite large tree specimens, and you might even consider buying and planting a suitable tree around which you could build this seat. The gently angled back follows the slope of the trunk, and the finished seat has been treated with a pale-coloured, non-toxic timber preservative to extend its life. Depending on the plan of your garden, you may want to treat it with preservative and then paint it to harmonize with your garden.

Finished timber sizes vary considerably, so it is very important to measure as you work.

CONSTRUCTION

First measure the circumference ('C') of the tree 450mm (18in) above ground level. Now calculate the inner length of the inner seat board ('S') by multiplying 'C' by 4 and dividing the total by 30; you can then calculate the total length of seat boards required by adding 150mm (6in) to 'S' and multiplying this new total by 24. The estimated total length of each row of backrest boards is simply 'C' measured at its appropriate height (that is, at the height of the trunk where the bottom edge of the backrest boards will fall). However, this is only a guide to calculating the amount of timber you will need to buy for the backrests; once the frames have been assembled and positioned around the tree, you will be able to measure the distance between the uprights to calculate the exact length.

Make a template, with angles as shown, cut from a 950 × 950mm (36 × 36in) sheet of plywood to aid cutting major parts and to act as a former during assembly.

The first job is to cut the uprights to length using the template: cut the bottoms at an angle so the uprights will slope backwards, notch out for the seat-support brace and rebate the top for the backrest support. Mark the height of the spar (horizontal seat support) and shape the top of the upright. This detailing is just a nice finishing touch, and if you don't feel confident about shaping the top of the upright as shown you could simply round off the front corner.

Place the spar on your template and mark and cut the angle necessary to fit the inside face of the spar flush against the upright.

Angle for seat board ends

305mm

$22\frac{1}{2}°$

38mm

125mm

$67\frac{1}{2}°$

Spar

45°

Brace

Upright

457mm

75mm

DRAWING UP A TEMPLATE

Use the template to mark a 22½-degree angle across the width of one of the seat board planks. Measure the hypotenuse, multiply by 3 (for three seat boards per section) and add 25mm (1in), which will allow for the 12mm (½in) spaces between each of the boards, to give the distance from the front to the back of the seat section.

Having calculated that measurement, position the upright and the spar on your template, then position the seat batten over the spar and carefully mark a rebate at one end of the seat batten to fit around the upright. Next, mark the front-to-back measure of the seat section along from the bottom of the seat batten; cut the batten to length, angling the front end at 67½ degrees. Cut a second batten that is the mirror image of the first.

SIDE AND FRONT ELEVATIONS

KEY TO SIDE AND FRONT ELEVATIONS

1 Upright – 75 × 75mm (3 × 3in)
2 Brace – 75 × 75mm (3 × 3in)
3 Seat Batten – 50 × 50mm (2 × 2in)
4 Spar – 50 × 75mm (2 × 3in)
5 Seat Boards – 32 × 138mm ($1\frac{1}{4} × 5\frac{1}{2}$in)
6 Backrest Boards – 38 × 138mm ($1\frac{1}{2} × 5\frac{1}{2}$in)
7 Backrest Support – 32 × 138mm ($1\frac{1}{4} × 5\frac{1}{2}$in)

**CUTTING THE BRACE NOTCH
IN THE UPRIGHT**

The backrest support can now be cut from 32 × 138mm ($1\frac{1}{4} \times 5\frac{1}{2}$in) softwood, to the length of the two backrest boards plus the 25mm (1in) gap between them; in this case, the backrest board is 300mm (12in) long. Chamfer the long edges of the support.

Cut all of the parts for the remaining seven frameworks. Carefully work around the pieces that you have already measured and cut for the first framework, and use them as templates for the corresponding parts. The project is now ready for assembly.

To assemble one of the seat sections, first fix the backrest supports to two of the uprights using two carriage bolts and nuts per support. Glue and screw two of the seat battens to the spar, one on either side, so that the bottoms of the battens are flush with the bottom of the spar; use three brass countersunk screws for each batten. Stagger the screws and make sure they are positioned below the centres of the seat boards.

Glue and screw the brace into the upright. Position the spar assembly on the brace and upright, and bolt

the spar assembly to the upright with two carriage bolts. Screw through the brace and up into the spar.

Make up five more frames in this way. The final two frames, for opposite sides, should be assembled without glue but with coach bolts securing the battens to the spar.

Although the front-to-back dimensions of the tree seat frames are pre-determined to take three seat boards per section, you will have to calculate the finished length of the slats yourself, since these depend on the size of the tree trunk around which you assemble the project. You have estimated this length already ('S'), but it is important that you check it accurately once the frames have been assembled and positioned.

Stand the eight frames round the tree, roughly in position and spaced apart at the required distance. Measure the length between two of the spars at the front of the uprights, and, back in your work space, mark this length (the revised, accurate 'S') on to one of the seat boards. Use the template to angle

CUTTING THE BRACE

Place the spar between the two seat battens so that the back end of the spar is flush with the start of the rebates and continue the angles from the front of the battens on to the front of the spar. Cut the front end of the spar so that it is V-shaped.

Next set the upright and the spar on the template to mark and cut the brace notches on each. The brace is notched into each by 25mm (1in) at its deepest point. The brace can now be cut to fit in the notches. The top on both sides of the brace must be rebated to take the seat battens.

**SHAPING THE ENDS OF
THE BACKREST BOARDS**

FITTING THE BACKREST BOARDS

triangle marked. To mark the angle across the thickness of the board, mark point 'B' 16mm ($\frac{5}{8}$in) in from 'A' on the top back edge of the board. Join point 'B' to point 'A' on the top front edge and to the bottom back corner. Cut away the waste. Angle all the ends of all the backrest boards in this way. Cut them out and screw them to the backrest supports.

Sand off any sharp corners and ensure that the whole seat is well protected with non-toxic exterior-grade wood preservative.

the ends outwards at 22$\frac{1}{2}$ degrees and cut out the seat board. Position the seat board between the seat battens of two frames. Allowing for a 12mm ($\frac{1}{2}$in) gap between the seat boards, measure the innermost lengths of the remaining two boards in this section, and angle the ends outwards as before. Cut these two boards out and position them between the seat battens to check that all three boards are an accurate fit. If necessary, plane down the edges of one or more of the boards so that they all fit snugly between the spars. Use these three boards as templates for all the others in the remaining sections (eight boards of each size).

Assemble two lots of three seat sections, drilling, countersinking and screwing the seat boards down into the seat battens. It is important that you place the bolted spars and battens so that they will be on opposite sides when the seat is in position. If you wish to remove the seat the battens can be unbolted from the spars. Mark on the ground

the positions of the eight uprights. It will be easier to level the seat if you dig holes – 150mm (6in) in diameter and 150mm (6in) deep – at the upright positions, and fill them with gravel. This will also provide good drainage, reducing the risk of the uprights rotting. Take the two seat sections and position them around the tree, then screw the final two sections of seat boards down into the seat battens as for the other sections.

The backrest boards taper towards the top. The ends of all the boards also need to be angled across their width and their thickness. Measure the length of each board at its widest point between the uprights and cut the board to this measure. At both ends, measure 100mm (4in) up from the bottom corner; at this point, measure 6mm ($\frac{1}{4}$in) in from the edge. Join this point to the bottom corner, continuing the line up to the top edge ('A'). Mark point 'A' on the opposite side of the top edge, draw a line down to the other bottom corner, and then cut out the

BASIC FRAME ASSEMBLY

Left: *Black iron hoops and the silver leaves of pyrus set up a fascinating dialogue that acts as a framework for the simple timber seats below. Brick paving provides a mellow floor, while the shallow step sets the area apart from the rest of the garden.*

Opposite above: *Wicker is always a great favourite in a garden, the perfect colour to tone with plants as well as being light enough to move around easily. Unfortunately the harsh creaking it sets up at the slightest movement is seldom conducive to a nap. That isn't a problem here as the seat is built from timber, the wicker acting as a shady bonnet.*

Opposite below: *In this unusual arbour, two mop-headed shrubs soften and front the vertical slats that form the main structure. Although the transition between light and shade is abrupt, there is enough dappled sun to prevent the composition from becoming sombre in its effect.*

SUN AND SHADE

In tropical and subtropical countries the light is far brighter than in temperate zones. Garden designers in places such as the Mediterranean and the Middle East have understood and exploited the juxtaposition of light and shade for centuries, making full use of the high drama that is available in such situations. You have only to walk along a Spanish street or through an Italian garden to appreciate this, not only in tonal values but in terms of temperature, shade offering release from the sometimes overpowering heat. Even in more northern countries, where the sun is lower in the sky and the light is altogether softer, the juxtaposition of sun and shade can still be used in rather more subtle ways to contribute to the design and charisma of a garden. The placing of a tree part way down a lawn, so that a long shadow is cast across the area, tends to increase the feeling of space, the shadow acting as a threshold between two different areas. If those areas are handled in different ways or styles then the effect is reinforced. This is a visual division but with no physical barrier whatsoever.

In practical terms, you will almost certainly want some areas that are either in full sun or total shade, both for people and plants. While sunny areas simply require an open position, shady retreats will involve the creation of an area in shadow, by whatever means. An obvious choice is in the shade cast by a building or a group of trees, while a whole range of garden constructions such as overhead beams, pergolas and arbours can produce rather more subtle effects as well as specific focal points within the garden framework.

In general terms the more open the framework the less dense the shade, and the dappled light cast in this way can often be the most attractive. The deeper the shade the greater the drama, a pool of darkness allowing an onlooker little idea of what is inside while for someone within quite the opposite applies.

These ideas show just how readily you can exploit the elements to provide another design tool at your disposal. Use the elements with sensitivity and you can add a new dimension to your palette, making sunshine and shadow work to your advantage in your garden planning.

ARBOUR

This hexagonal arbour provides a delightfully shaded retreat in a corner of the garden. The trellis at the back is the perfect support for fragrant climbing roses and these have also scrambled over the roof. Such a building, being of an open construction, offers little resistance to the wind, so it must be firmly secured to the ground. The hexagonal shape of the design calls for a lot of complicated angling of the component parts, and the construction of this project is the most difficult in the book.

CONSTRUCTION

To set out a hexagon you will need to establish a centre point of the building. Each corner will be 760mm (30in) from the centre and this will allow you to fit 605mm (24in) wide panels of trellis to form the outside 'walls'. Each centre angle of a hexagon is 60 degrees.

To plot the hexagon, mark a circle with a radius of 760mm (30in) on the site you have chosen using a pencil on the end of a piece of string pegged at the centre of your plot. Choose a point on the circumference for the position of one of the posts, place the peg in the ground at this point, and draw out another circle, again 760mm (30in) in diameter, clearly marking the points at which it bisects the circumference of the original circle. Move the peg to one of the points and repeat the operation until the six post positions have been marked.

The main upright posts are cut from 100 × 100mm (4 × 4in) timber and can be set into steel sockets bolted to a solid base or into spiked post-supports that are driven into the ground. Make sure the proprietary spiked post-supports you buy have adjusting screws that allow the post to be checked for vertical with a spirit level and then cramped tightly in place. When driving spikes into the ground always check first for water pipes or electricity cables.

The uprights at the six corners of the arbour need to have slots in the top to accept the roof rafters. If you are unable to buy ready-made posts with slots in the top, mark out and cut a 50mm (2in) wide slot, 100mm (4in) deep, centred across one end of each of the six posts. Mark out the width of the slot using a marking

MARKING OUT THE SITE

SHAPING THE CENTRE POST

**TIE-BEAM AND
CENTRE POST ASSEMBLY**

gauge, saw down 100mm (4in) using a tenon saw, and chisel out the waste. The upright posts should be approximately 2.15m (7ft) high, but remember to allow for the depth of the fixing socket, if this is the method you are using. Nail 45-degree mouldings along the lengths of the uprights to allow fixing of trellis panels. The mouldings should run along the lengths of the posts finishing just short of the bottoms to fit in the sockets or spiked supports. Glue and nail the mouldings in place on both faces that have not had the slot cut down them, so that they finish about half way across the width of the posts. Set the posts in the support sockets, with the mouldings towards the 'interior' of the arbour, and cramp together tightly.

A tie-beam between two opposite uprights will give the building strength and stability. Cut the tie-beam to length from 100 × 50mm (4 × 2in) with rebates at either end to fit over the uprights. The tie-beam should span between two opposite uprights, finishing 25mm (1in) short of the outside edges of the uprights. At either end of the tie-beam, cut a 75 × 25mm (3 × 1in) rebate. Angle the ends of the tie-beam above the uprights at 45 degrees to accept the rafters. Mark the centre of the tie-beam on the bottom edge and fix with carriage bolts and nuts between the uprights.

Cut a notch in two of the rafters so that they will fit over the corner posts. Loosely bolt the rafters in position over the tie-beam, crossing at the apex. Support the pair of rafters with a G cramp and set the angle of the rafters to 45 degrees to the tie-beam. Mark a line on both rafters where they cross over.

SHAPING THE RAFTERS

Planing the top

Angled end

Take the rafters down and mark vertical lines at the cross-over points; these will be at 45 degrees to the edges. Ensure that both rafters are marked to the same length and cut the vertical ends. Replace the rafters on the posts so that the vertical faces come together at the centre. Measure from the bottom edge of the centre of the tie-beam to the apex of the roof (where the rafters now meet): this gives the length for the centre post.

Cut the centre post to length from 100×100mm (4×4in). The centre post needs to be shaped to a regular hexagon in cross section so that the rafters will neatly butt against it at the apex of the roof. Mark the position for a 50×50mm (2×2in) rafter centrally on one side of the centre post. On the opposite side of the centre post mark a line 12mm ($\frac{1}{2}$in) in from and parallel with the edge. Mark the position for a rafter centrally along this line. On the adjacent faces, mark a point 43mm ($1\frac{3}{4}$in) along ('A' on Shaping the Centre Post, page 49) and join this point first to the edges of where the first rafter will fall, and then to the point where the edges of the rafter will fall when you have sawn and planed away the waste 12mm ($\frac{1}{2}$in). You should now have drawn the edges of a regular hexagon. Plane or saw the face angles so that the post is hexagonal in cross section. At the bottom of the centre post, cut a slot to fit over the tie-beam, making sure that it runs between opposite flat faces of the hexagon.

Measure the distance between opposite faces of the centre post and divide by two. Mark and cut this distance vertically, from the upper ends of the two rafters so that they butt on to the centre post at the same angle. Use these rafters to mark, cut and shape the remaining four rafters. Plane chamfers on the top edges and cut the bottom ends to a 120-degree V shape so that the fascia boards (which are added later) will fit flush against the ends of the rafters.

Replace the rafters at either end of the tie-beam and position the centre post on the centre of the tie-beam, between the rafters. Nail through the rafters into the centre post. Drill and bolt through the uprights into the rafters. Position a block on either side of the bottom of the centre post and nail through the blocks into the top of the tie-beam

PLAN OF CORNER DETAIL

1   Trellis panel frame

2   Half round moulding

3   45 degree moulding

4   Slotted upright –
    100×100mm (4×4in)

5   Tie-beam (angled at the end
    to accept the rafter) –
    100×50mm (4×2in)

FIXING THE RAFTERS AND FASCIA BOARD

Rafter

Tie-beam

Upright

Fascia board

angles for the boards in situ, so that they will fit from the centre line of one rafter to the next. Lay the boards from the bottom upwards, pinning through the bottom of one board into the top of the preceding board it overlaps.

Such a pretty building as this deserves a decorative top-knot: nail a post cap and finial to the top of the centre post.

Chamfer the inside faces of the trellis panel frames so that they fit snugly between the 45-degree mouldings. Nail them in place and cover the gaps at the outside corners with half round mouldings.

As an optional extra you might think of fitting a slatted seat inside the arbour: screw 150mm (6in) angle brackets to the inner faces of the uprights, and lay two 75 × 50mm (3 × 2in) boards between them. Cut the ends of the boards to a 60 degree angle so that they finish square to the centre line of the corner posts, and screw them in place. Treat all the surfaces with a non-toxic, exterior-grade wood preservative. Allow this to dry, then paint or finish as required.

ADDING THE ROOF BOARDS

Cut boards in situ

to keep the centre beam in place. Do not, however, nail the centre post to the tie-beam.

The remaining rafters can now be positioned, bolting them to the uprights and nailing them to the appropriate face of the centre post.

Fascia boards surround the top of the structure below the roof and these can now be cut to length. Angle the ends at 60 degrees inwards so that they neatly butt together. Nail the fascia boards to the shaped ends of the rafters.

The roof is clad in 12mm (½in) feather-edged boards pinned to the rafters. You will need to chamfer the undersides of the angled edges so that each board abutts with those either side of it. Mark the cutting

PLAN VIEW OF ROOF

DECORATIVE DIVIDERS

*A garden, of whatever size, that can be seen at a glance is far
less interesting than one divided into separate areas.
As you move from space to space, the garden seems to unfold
with a satisfying element of mystery and surprise.
In all probability the area will also feel larger than it really is,
since you can spend time absorbing the character
of each component part before moving on to the next.
This technique has been used in the design of many great and
famous gardens and, although your backyard may be
considerably smaller, the principle remains much the same.*

*This simple, flower-laden trellis
sits on top of a low brick wall
that part-straddles the garden.
Such a divider is particularly
effective as it lets you catch
a tantalizing glimpse of the
'room' beyond, making it
all the more attractive.*

Right: *Gates may be enticing or welcoming; the character of the gate sets the theme. This strong timber design, now beautifully mellowed with age, is distinctly rural and the old brick path and hedge reinforce the country garden feel. The positioning of a single white foxglove provides a point of emphasis, brightening the plain green foliage in the background.*

Far right: *Gardens don't have to be dull in winter. The tonal contrasts in this snow-covered garden are delicious and sharp. The gate invites you to explore beyond and creates a delicate filigree against the white lawn. The two yew buttresses capped with snow resemble Christmas puddings or ice-cream cones. Imagination is one of the great delights of gardening; make sure you use it.*

Space division within a garden is a vital tool in the creation of separate 'rooms'. Walls, screens and fences can be used in many ways to produce a variety of effects, so you should consider carefully what you want from your design. Two walls coming together to form a narrow opening will create a build-up of tension, or expectancy, as you approach the gap and a subsequent release, or feeling of surprise, as the next space is entered. A curving trellis, gently leading you through a garden, but preventing you from seeing beyond the next corner, engenders mystery. A partly open gate is an invitation to find more.

Dividers can be constructed from various materials, and each has a character and suitability that makes it more or less appropriate for a given location. The choice is often confusing, given the vast range of options available, but certain guidelines, followed sensibly, will narrow down the options and ensure success.

One important rule is that the materials you use should reflect those used elsewhere in the composition. If your house is of brick or stone,

the natural choice, funds permitting, will be to use the same material in the garden. Although walls are expensive, if well built, on suitable foundations and of adequate thickness, they will last for generations and be an ideal host for all kinds of climbing plants. Remember that, almost without exception, the real thing is better than an imitation. Reconstituted stone always looks just that, while the ubiquitous concrete 'screen block' or pierced wall is appalling in most situations. The simplest things usually work best, particularly if the divider will not necessarily be seen as a feature in its own right but as part of a larger scheme.

Timber is a most versatile material and can be fashioned into the simplest fence or the most exotic trellis. Its life-span is less than brick or stone, but if thoroughly coated with non-toxic preservative or bought already pressure-treated it will last for many years. Other advantages are its suitability for self-build projects and the relatively low purchase price. Weight, too, is a consideration: timber, being light, is an ideal

Far left: *A good feature in its own right can look quite out of place in the wrong setting. This sleek, modern trellis archway is, for my taste, at odds with the cottage feel of the herb and vegetable garden beyond. The chic formality of the trellis competes with the mellow, basketweave brick path – both beautiful features, but not complementary ones.*

Left: *Black, or dark colours, absorb light; white and other light colours actively reflect it, providing a much better screen. The shadow patterns set up by sunlight filtering through this trellis are delightful, while the hooped shape increases the apparent height of the feature. A hanging basket bursting with fuchsias draws attention to the curved ceiling and contrasts with the soft green of the ferns at ground level.*

choice for a roof garden, where it is a suitable material for screens that will filter rather than obstruct the wind, as well as for overhead beams and raised beds.

Hedges will be cheaper than both stone walls and timber but, on the debit side, take longer to establish and need clipping to keep in shape. Having said that, once established, a well-tended hedge can provide a perfect 'green wall'. Whether trimmed with a horizontal or curved top, or formed into balls or finials to emphasize a gateway, hedges act as one of the most attractive backdrops to planting, and their shape and height can be modified as you wish.

Of course, screens are not always simply decorative features. They can be used as practical devices to hide a utility area, store dustbins or form the boundary of the vegetable garden. Such screens should never be planned or positioned in isolation. It is better to extend them to link with the wider garden pattern, so that problem areas are genuinely disguised without becoming eyecatchers in their own right.

Another way to make full use of dividers is to give them a dual or changing role. A stout timber archway could start life as a child's swing, with access to the remainder of the garden temporarily re-routed. Later, when the swing is no longer needed, you could realign the path and let the feature take on a new character as a support for climbers. Such a scheme would be ideal in a small garden where play space might be limited. The requirements of a family garden change with the years and it is a good idea, therefore, to make versatility one of your prime considerations when you are planning a project.

Raised beds can also be used to create divisions and separate areas. They tend to act as lower-level barriers, although the contents of the bed will also affect the degree of screening. Raised beds can be used in many places, but are often most effective around the perimeter of a patio where they help to contain a space, or flanking steps that lead from one area to another. The hard edges of raised beds can be softened by growing plants that trail over the sides.

TRELLIS

Trellis, or treillage as it is sometimes pompously called, has a long pedigree as a garden feature. In its original form, it probably consisted of a woven screen of branches used for fencing or to support trained fruit trees against a wall. Today it is primarily used as a decorative element, but with careful planning you can combine this with the traditional approach to produce a very attractive screen, wind-break or base for climbing plants.

The most widely used type of trellis consists of thin strips of wood nailed together to form a diamond or squared pattern, but there are many other possibilities. Plastic is increasingly available and, if of good quality and simple design, can be quite acceptable. Wire, steel and wrought-iron have long been used in a variety of ways, ranging from strands of wire stretched between posts to delicate filigrees that reflect the architecture of an adjoining building. One of the great advantages of free-standing trellis is, of course, the ease with which it can be erected.

Pre-assembled trellis can be attached to posts that have been simply slotted into metal sleeves, or the posts can be spiked and driven into the ground or securely concreted into position. The initial cost may be high but, if regularly maintained, such a feature will last a life-time.

A quick look at your local garden centre will give you an idea of the enormous variety of trellis styles available. This is because trellis has become fashionable of late, so it is often used for that reason alone – an approach that seldom reflects good design sense. High fashion also comes with an expensive price tag, and many suppliers produce catalogues offering pseudo-bespoke designs that cost a small fortune. To justify the price, the patterns are often vastly complicated, and this makes them very difficult to fit into an overall garden composition. There is, of course, a place for the complicated and intricate, but that place has to be reflected elsewhere in the design. Remember the prime rule that 'simple things work best' and you will not go far wrong.

One of the most common uses for trellis is as a support for climbers against a free-standing wall or against a house. In fact, wiring with horizontal strands is often more effective in this situation,

Simple white diamond trellis is the perfect foil to a fresh green climber, the underlying pattern providing background stability to the sun-speckled leaves.

Opposite above left: A white background to squared trellis appears to reduce the height of this wall, setting the upper limit of the 'room'. Such trellis is also an ideal support for potted plants, which can be hooked on to the horizontal slats.

Opposite above right: False-perspective trellis, or trompe-l'oeil as it is often called, seldom fools anyone – but it is fun. It is also the obvious focus for a well-chosen ornament such as this handsomely planted bowl.

Opposite below left: A simple free-standing device is an excellent host to any climber, either decorative or edible. The overall effect is charming and functional, the construction is minimal, and the fish above the apex of the triangular supports adds a restrained element of humour.

Opposite below right: When covered with planting, a divider like this one will prevent the eye from running the full length of a border, helping to create a feeling of suspense and drawing your view further down the garden. Instead of unwieldy fence posts, neat lengths of angle iron have been driven into the ground to support the panel ends.

costing less and involving little maintenance. Trellis may look better if it sets out to become a decorative element in its own right. Properly chosen and fitted, trellis will brighten and break the line of a dull wall. Make sure you align the tops of the panels with any obvious features such as windows or doors and remember that you will need to maintain it regularly, even when pre-treated timber is used. The plants which are growing against the trellis will have to be untied and any dead foliage cut away first. It can be difficult to remove climbers which have woven their way through the slats, and this may prove a maintenance problem.

Further down the garden, trellis can make an ideal screen, either in a decorative role, allowing you to catch a glimpse of what is beyond, or in a more practical way as a visual barrier to a utility or other area. The simplest pattern of trellis is often the best at hiding an unattractive view or feature. Climbers can be planted to complete the screen; if evergreens are chosen then the feature will remain effective and attractive even during the winter months.

Decorative screens can either be completely straightforward or rather more complicated. In an uncluttered, domestic garden a basic squared pattern of strong trellis will be ideal. This style is excellent for climbers and will easily withstand the wear and tear caused by children and teenagers playing ball in the garden. It could extend part way across the space or include an archway to the area beyond. In the context of a more stylized and formal garden, there is justification for a more complex pattern. Here, a trellis could follow shapes used elsewhere, with curved tops, hooped arches or close-set slats combined in any number of ways. Remember, too, that trellis is internationally used. Superb styles have been developed in Japan, the Far East and other parts of the world, extending the vast catalogue of design possibilities.

Another practical approach to screens and dividers is to use them as wind-breaks. Very often a solid fence or wall will create wind turbulence on the lee-side. In contrast, slats or trellis tend to filter the wind effectively with no such disadvantages. This facility can be exploited both at ground level and in a roof garden, which is where trellis will really come into its own.

Far left: *Trellis need not simply be used for dividers and screens in the further reaches of the garden. Here it makes a simple but effective support for climbers around a porch. A design like this one casts little shadow and provides an attractive and simple welcome to the house.*

Top left: *Close-mesh diamond trellis is the ideal boundary for a rooftop garden. It is lightweight and will filter the wind far more effectively than a solid structure. In this design the pattern has been continued in the raised bed, with planting chosen to soften the outline.*

Bottom left: *This custom-built design in well-made, solid timber is the perfect divider between two outdoor 'rooms'. The squares are slightly larger than usual and combine well with the hooped pattern that gives the feature a real feeling of movement. Climbers and planting at a lower level have been well chosen, tempering the architectural line of the screen.*

GARDEN DIVIDER

This divider is cheap and easy to build, provides an increasingly effective screen for the building opposite as the climbers develop, accentuates the slight change of level and, finally, separates the more formal part of the garden from the lawn.

Fixed to the exterior wall of a house, the divider works as an architectural link between inside and outside, but such a feature could easily be modified so that it is a freestanding unit. The rebate in the top rail above the left-hand intermediate post is not essential at this point because the fixing to the wall is providing rigidity, but if the feature is built to be freestanding then all the posts must be rebated into the top rail.

The size of this divider could be varied to suit individual situations; in this garden it is approximately 2m (6ft 6in) high.

**CORNER OF
LATTICE PANEL (F)**

**END POST AND
TOP RAIL (C)**

CONSTRUCTION

First of all construct the framework for the diagonal lattice from 50 × 50mm (2 × 2in) softwood with halving joints at the corners. Check that the frames are square and glue and nail them together.

Mark out the position of the slats on the framework with about a 75mm (3in) spacing between each. Cut the slats to length with a 45-degree angle at each end (mark the angle using a mitre block or

INTERMEDIATE POST AND TOP RAIL (B)

adjustable set square). Glue and nail the slats to the framework with one nail at each end at right angles to the slats and at a corresponding angle to the frame. You will find it easiest if you work from opposite corners towards the centre of the lattice panel.

Offer up the main post to the wall of the house, check for vertical and mark the position for three expanding masonry bolts. Remove the post and bore the holes in it. Offer up the post again and mark the position of the holes on the masonry. Drill these using a masonry bit to a depth slightly greater than the distance the bolt will penetrate the wall. Bolt the post to the house,

END POST CONCRETED IN PLACE (G)

fitting spacers to keep the upright slightly away from the wall of the building.

Cut the top rail to the right length: that is, so that it will span the length of both lattice panels, the archway and the four posts. Cut rebates to accept the posts into the rail at the appropriate positions.

Take the top rail and position it at the base of the fixed post to mark the position of the other end post on the ground. Cut a gauge batten to the same length as the top rail, minus the width of two posts, and mark on the gauge batten the intermediate post positions.

Dig holes for the intermediate posts and end post. Cut the end post so that 450mm (18in) will be set in the ground and set the post on a 100mm (4in) layer of well-compacted hardcore. Prop the post upright with long battens set on two adjacent sides. Set the top rail in position to check that the spacing is correct; check the spacing at the bottom using the gauge batten.

**NAILING LATTICE PANEL TO
FENCE BRACKET (E)**

Cut the intermediate posts to length, fill the holes with a 100mm (4in) layer of well-rammed hardcore, check the post heights and prop upright. Concrete the posts in position, bringing the surface slightly clear of the ground. Allow two or three days for the concrete to dry, then remove the props.

Nail or screw fence-post brackets to the inside faces of the pairs of posts, level with the top and bottom of the diagonal lattice panels. The bottoms of the panels should be just clear of the ground. Slide the panels up into the brackets at the top and then ease them down into the bottom ones. Nail the panels in place.

**VERTICAL AND HORIZONTAL
TRELLIS RAILS (D)**

To protect the top of the lattice panels, fit rails along their lengths. These can be measured and cut along with the trellis sections on either side of the arch. Nail through the vertical trellis rail into the end horizontal trellis rail and up through the capping rail (before it is fixed down) into the end of the vertical rail.

Nail through the top rail and the intermediate posts into the ends of the trellis rails. Finally, nail through the capping rail into the lattice panel top frame.

BOLTING MAIN POST TO WALL (A)

Left: *An arch or pergola should always be integrated with the design of the garden. This simple arrangement frames a grass path that in turn has a statue as a focal point at the end. The arch is all the more telling as it sets up a visual dialogue with the rose-garlanded rope swags.*

Opposite: *This gloriously unkempt combination of path and pergola has in fact been very carefully designed to lead both foot and eye through a cool tunnel towards the informal steps and sunlit turf beyond. The square timber supports are topped by simple poles that span the walkway and provide support for fragrant roses climbing up and overhead. The apparently haphazard planting simply heightens the intended effect of a delightful rural idyll.*

PERGOLAS

Pergolas are one of the oldest garden elements. Their history can be traced back to the very earliest representations of cultivation in Egyptian courtyards. Their role was a dual one: to support the twining stems of vines and to provide a degree of shelter from the all-pervading sun. Since then, pergolas, tunnels and arches have been incorporated into many different types of garden, but it is worth remembering that a pergola is primarily a vehicle for plants. Climbers in particular often thrive on a pergola, growing far better than they do when planted close to the house, where their growth is hindered by foundations, poor soil or the lack of moisture caused by an adjoining wall's 'rain shadow'.

In contemporary design terms, a pergola will tend to be a dominant element, particularly in a relatively small space, and its positioning and method of construction will play an important part in the overall garden pattern. The height and shape of a pergola make it naturally attractive, so it should be sited to draw both foot and eye in a particular direction. If it is built to follow the curve of a path, the far end will disappear with an air of mystery. If it is straight, the focal point might be a well-chosen statue, an urn or a seat. Whatever the focus and wherever the destination, it should be positive – a pergola placed at random is simply wasted space.

Styles and methods of construction vary enormously, from simple timber affairs, through complicated brick, stone or tile piers to metal arches that are virtually hidden when garlanded with climbers. As with paving and walling, the theme should be taken from the surrounding environment. A brick-built pergola adjacent to a stone cottage would look incongruous. In a contemporary setting a modern pergola will be appropriate. I recently designed a superb pergola from a series of hoops of large-diameter tubular stainless steel. The final effect of the metal glittering through a tracery of foliage was incredibly dramatic, confirming my belief that, ancient or modern, a properly used and sensitively sited pergola will always be an indispensable element in good garden design.

BEAN SUPPORT

This feature is genuinely versatile and could act as a screen at the corner of a terrace, a container on a terrace or set as a pair to flank the entrance to a vegetable area. Even a moderate wind could easily topple a structure this tall, so stability is extremely important, and the main posts must be firmly driven into the ground.

CONSTRUCTION
Level the site and mark out the position of the trough, using pegs driven into the ground at the corners and at the positions of the intermediate posts. Join together with twine, making sure corners are at right angles. Bore holes for the two main upright posts 450mm (18in) deep, or drive in 600mm (24in) long steel post sockets. If doing this, check for the position of any underground services such as water pipes or electricity cables.

800mm

245mm

400mm

300mm

**MARKING OUT THE SITE
AND POST POSITIONS**

*Cut the posts so that they will
extend about 1800mm (72in) above
ground level, and offer them up to
the holes or sockets. Adjust so that
the tops of the post are level.*

*Remove the posts from the holes and
lay them down flat, spaced at the
distance they will be when erected.
Lay the bottom support batten at
the bottom of the posts with an
equal overlap at either end and
mark the position of the inside faces
of posts on the batten. These marks
can then be transferred centrally to
the cross beams for the top of the
posts. Drill countersunk clearance
holes for No 12 screws in the cross
beams staggered on the posts and
38mm (1½in) from the top and
bottom edges of where the cross
beams will be positioned.*

*Angle the post tops at 45 degrees so
water will easily run clear.*

*Line up the post marks on one cross
beam against the two posts, and
cramp the cross beam to the posts
using 'G' cramps so the top is flush
with the post top. Drill pilot holes
and screw the cross beam to the
posts using two 62mm (2½in) No 12
brass countersunk screws either end.
Repeat for the other beam.*

*Drill countersunk clearance holes at
600mm (24in) centres in the top
string support batten. Make a
template from an off-cut of 6mm
(¼in) plywood to mark the nail*

*positions. Use slightly blunted 38mm
(1½in) galvanized nails, and drive
these in a staggered pattern so the
batten is not split. Screw the batten
centrally to the front cross beam,
12mm (½in) up from the bottom
edge with 60mm (2½in) No 8 brass
countersunk woodscrews.*

350mm

150 × 25mm
cross beam

FIXING THE CROSS BEAMS

*Stagger nails or screws into the
bottom string support as above.
Mark the ground level on the posts.
Screw the batten centrally to the
front of the posts, 250mm (10in)
above ground level. Use 60mm
(2½in) No 8 countersunk brass screws.*

*Knot garden twine between the top
and bottom nails, or use plastic-
coated wire, neatly tied off.*

*Lift the frame into the holes or
sockets and set in concrete or tap
home as appropriate.*

75 × 75mm post

FIXING THE STRING SUPPORT BATTENS

*With the frame in position you can
start on the troughs. Drive in one
corner post so the top finishes
285mm (11½in) above ground level.
Check for vertical and drive in the
remaining corner and intermediate
posts to follow the lines marked out
with pegs. Level the tops from the
first post using a straight edge and
spirit level. Check that the lower
string support batten does not
protrude beyond the end corner
posts of the trough.*

*Screw the boards for the troughs to
the corner posts and intermediate
posts with 60mm (2½in) No 8 brass*

**SCREWING TROUGH BOARDS
TO THE CORNER POSTS**

38 × 38mm
corner post

75 × 25mm boards

*screws, two per post. Check that the
bottom boards are horizontal before
fixing the remaining boards. Stagger
the ends of the boards. Any ends
that protrude can be cut off flush
when screwed in position.
Finally, treat all of the timber
thoroughly with two coats of a
non-toxic wood preservative.*

RAISED BEDS

I'm essentially a lazy gardener and if there is a way to tend plants at a comfortable height, rather than at ground level, then I'm all for it. But this is just one of the advantages of raised-bed gardening. Raised beds give young plants a much-needed boost, soften the hard line of an adjoining wall, can double as occasional seats, become an integral part of steps or ramps or temporarily provide a children's sand-pit. You can use them to contain a given area such as a patio or vegetable garden, and remember that the soil in a raised bed can be quite different from that in another part of the garden. This will allow you to grow plants that would not normally thrive in the immediate vicinity – for example ericaceous plants could be grown in an acidic bed in an otherwise chalky garden.

Opposite above left: This stone raised bed forms part of a rockery and fulfils its function perfectly, elevating the delicate alpine planting to a handy working height and also bringing it closer to eye-level.

Opposite above right: Railway sleepers are ideal for garden construction. They're easy to lay and almost indestructable – but don't try to move them alone as they're very heavy and need a person at either end for easy lifting. Here, the contrast in colour between the dark wood and the lighter gravel path is particularly effective.

Opposite below: Sleepers have been cut into short sections and set vertically to form an attractive bed. Burying approximately 50 per cent of the length below ground level makes the feature immensely strong. Varying the height of the tops sets up an interesting rhythm, with plants arranged to blur the outline.

To exploit their full potential, you should consider the option of raised beds during the initial stages of creating your garden design. Where you decide to put them will of course have a bearing on the materials you use for their construction. A brick raised bed could echo brick paving, which in turn takes its cue from the house. Stone will combine well with stone, timber with timber and so on. But this is only a guide and these rules can be broken. Neatly laid railway sleepers look superb in a contemporary setting adjoining a house built from brick. Similarly, rendered concrete blocks with a neat precast slab coping would offer an immediate visual affinity with a stuccoed building.

If beds are built with solid brick or stone walls then drainage will be necessary to prevent the soil from becoming waterlogged. You can leave a number of open vertical joints close to the ground to allow excess water to seep away. Alternatively, drainage pipes can be neatly incorporated at a similar level, but make sure that they finish flush with the face of the wall. As with any wall, suitable concrete foundations are essential. Most importantly, a raised bed should never be built directly on top of existing paving. Remember, too, that raised beds may cause damp problems if built against a house wall. Always leave a gap between a bed and an adjoining wall.

Timber is an excellent choice of material and very versatile. Beds can utilize logs set vertically into the ground or laid horizontally, nailed into supporting battens or posts set into the ground on the inside of the bed. Large timber plant boxes, constructed from boards and filled with lightweight compost, will be ideal for roof gardens, where weight considerations mean that heavier materials are not suitable.

Left: This curved brick wall with a neat stone coping echoes the brick paving used in the patio. The smothering flowers and foliage soften the effect and inject an element of contrast. Such a raised bed could exist alone or make up part of an altogether larger scheme of retaining walls and different levels.

Right: *In this classic combination, hedge and gate sit comfortably together, the sharp pickets seeming to push the green arch up and away from the entrance. A hedge like this takes a while to establish and needs careful clipping and training during its development, but the end result is worth it and would provide a real welcome to any garden.*

Opposite above: *Fence, screen or both – the definition hardly matters as this is a delightful way to divide the space. White roses provide a perfect contrast, sparkling against the soft green background. It is worth remembering that, while rustic timbers look fine in the more distant parts of a garden, they may appear uncomfortable if situated close to the house, particularly as they have a limited life-span and tend to rot.*

Opposite below: *Ivy covers this brick wall, growing tightly against the surface and needing minimal maintenance to keep it neat. Holes clipped in the foliage introduce a textured effect with a contrast between light and shadow. The ivy-clad birdbath is also very effective: you need to look twice to see how it works.*

FENCES, GATES AND HEDGES

Fences and hedges can form either internal divisions or the external boundaries of your plot. Gates will always be the ins and outs of a garden. As with many of the other elements of the design, the range of options is enormous, but here again your choice should reflect the general style of the surrounding composition so that the development of your garden has continuity.

In many cases the choice between a fence and a hedge can be an entirely subjective one. A fence is quickly erected, offers immediate screening and has an average life of between 10 and 15 years. Options can range from the soft texture of woven stems of hazel or willow to the austerity of a purpose-designed pattern of carefully shaped and spaced slats. There will certainly be a requirement for maintenance, either by regular painting or treatment with a non-toxic preservative. Cost will vary, but any fence, even if home-built, will involve a considerable outlay both in materials and in labour. This being the case, it is important to consider all the possibilities when planning the fencing most suitable for your garden.

Hedges are initially far cheaper to buy and plant, but will take several, or in some cases many, years to reach maturity and provide an adequate screen. In visual terms they offer a far softer appearance than a fence or wall and often provide the perfect backdrop to planting, seating or statuary. Because you are dealing with a living material, the appearance of a hedge will change with time, whilst, of course, it can be trained or clipped into a variety of patterns and shapes. Topiary is a fascinating art, and the element of humour it adds to a garden design is invaluable. Remember, though, that a lot of maintenance is required to keep a clipped shape, with its crisp edges, looking trim, but that this is essential if the impact of your topiary is not to be lost.

Gates provide a natural focal point at the end of paths and paving. The choice is legion, ranging from a low, open structure of woven iron to a full-height timber door that will exclude the view completely. Choose carefully, remembering that gates are often the first thing that visitors see – and first impressions count.

WATER FEATURES

*Water has a magic all its own – from the strict formality
of a rectangular pool set within paving and sculptural planting,
to the sweep of an irregularly shaped pond that sets up
reflections of everything around it.
Imagine the crash of a waterfall on to rocks below
or the gentle murmur of a fountain in a raised bed. The mood of
water changes too: steel grey, sharp and rimed with frost
in the depths of winter; deliciously cool and
framed with aquatic planting in the warmth of summer.
Of course, water features are not just appreciated by us: a pool
is one of the richest habitats you can create in your garden.
Birds and insects will come to drink, the frogs and
toads that are great predators of unruly bugs will thrive,
marginals and deep water plants will bring their own exotic
charm, while fish complete the picture.
More than any other feature, water will echo your personality.
Just how you handle it will be a subtle challenge –
success brings enormous pleasure.*

*This circular pool is a natural
focus in a courtyard setting. It is
raised, bringing it closer to
eye-level and making it a good
deal safer for young children.
It's also at a perfect height for
sitting on, whilst the blue brick
coping matches that used in
the surrounding raised beds.*

Left: In this tiny formal pool a cherub spouts water endlessly into the air. Clipped pyramids of box heighten the formality of the design, while the simple pattern of basketweave brick paving forms a mellow floor. Although the composition is certainly pretty, the combination of a small pool and high fountain may not be practical, as the wind tends to catch the spray, emptying the pool in a relatively short time.

Opposite: *While it is impossible to create a true Japanese garden outside Japan, this design interprets a number of the classic elements of Oriental garden composition in a subtle and sympathetic way. Timber has been extensively used in the bridge and decking, with bamboo forming the handrail and the surrounding fencing. The pool lining has been painted black to give an impression of depth and is sufficiently large to support a thriving population of fish and other aquatic life.*

Since a water feature can be the making or breaking of a garden, you should plan it carefully. As with other areas of design, the simple things invariably work the best. I so often visit gardens where a 'Geneva' fountain gushes high into the air from a quite minuscule pond. Apart from being completely out of scale, the combination is totally impractical, as spray drift results in an alarming rate of water loss in even the lightest of winds.

The style of a pool should reflect the character of the area around it. A pond set within a patio can be built from the same material as the paving, interlocking perhaps with a raised bed or set within the angle of a wall. The further away from the house you get, the softer and looser the composition can become, and this change can be reflected in the shape of the pool.

The situation with regard to sun and shade will also be important. Try to find a position well out in the open, away from the shadow and leaf fall of overhanging trees. If leaves are a problem – and neighbours' trees are often to blame as much as yours – then spread a light net over the pool at the onset of autumn. You can then remove the whole lot once they have all fallen.

In the ideal pool there is such a balance of aquatic plants, fish, water snails and a host of other insect life that the fish hardly ever need feeding. There are now specialist water garden centres where you can buy all that is necessary to bring your pool alive. If you let them know the size and depth of your pool they will work out the correct permutations, down to the last water snail that will help to keep the water clear. The smaller the area the more difficult it is to create a balanced habitat. The minimum size for a pool is 1.8 × 1.8m (6 × 6ft), while 450mm (18in) is an adequate depth. You will also need a shelf or ledge, approximately 220mm (9in) below the surface and about 300mm (12in) wide, on which to stand marginal plants.

In the past all garden pools were made from concrete. This made them time-consuming to create and fraught with the problems of hair-line cracks. Tough plastic and butyl liners have provided the solution and are now available in virtually any size and in many different grades. An alternative option is to choose a rigid or semi-rigid pool. But, although these can be quickly and easily installed, they are often rather too small to be really effective.

FORMAL PONDS

A formal pattern suggests symmetry in which one side or part of a garden or design is identical to the other. While this is not always strictly true, we tend to think of a formal design as one that is built up from geometric elements rather than free-form shapes, displaying a strong degree of visual control and stability.

As far as pools are concerned, the geometry can be square, rectangular, circular, triangular or even a combination of these elements. Formal ponds are usually surrounded by a coping of some kind, even if they are set within an area of soft landscaping in the form of lawn or planting. They may form a set-piece within the larger setting of a courtyard, sunken garden or parterre, and will associate particularly well with decorative features such as statuary, topiary or regularly placed urns and ornaments.

You may want to use an ornament as the centrepiece of the pool itself. Figures engaged in some sort of watery activity are very popular, as are bowls from which water overflows back into the pool below. Where a pool is backed by a wall there is the opportunity to fit a mask that also spouts water. Lions' heads are the most common, but are rarely modelled well and tend to become a design cliché. Instead try and seek out something different: a gargoyle or a face of some other kind could be a better choice and could inject a humorous touch into the formality of the composition. As well as being visually pleasing, a fountain or cascade adds a further dimension to the attractions of a formal pool, with the sound of falling water providing a soothing background to garden activities. A variety of effects can be produced, depending on the type of fountain jet or head fitted.

Any pond including a fountain or cascade will require a pump. Today there is a wide range of submersible types available that are easily fitted within the pool itself. Many work from a 12 volt supply that is connected back to a transformer inside the house or garage. When using electricity in the garden, and particularly near water, make absolutely sure that all connections are of the correct weatherproof type and employ a qualified electrician to install the pump so that you can be absolutely sure that it is safe.

Opposite above: *In design terms a square is completely static and as such makes an ideal centrepiece in a formal situation. The effect of this pool is heightened by the stepped brickwork that leads the eye down to the water. The hummocks of box, the carefully positioned pots, seat and trained ivy all add to the overall geometric arrangement of this well-planned area.*

Opposite below: *A water-filled bowl and fountain draw the eye to the centre of this composition. Crisp brick paving surrounds the pool which is in turn softened by the formally placed beds and the dense evergreen background. If you are planning to use a bowl in this way you should first make sure that it is completely frost-proof and able to withstand the ravages of winter.*

Left above: *A tiny circular pool introduces a note of formality in an otherwise rural garden. Well-laid coping acts as a mowing edge to the surrounding lawn, but the lily plants will need thinning regularly if they are not to overrun the pool area completely.*

Left below: *Fountains and bubble jets are fine, but you will never enjoy the beauty of reflections from such a disturbed surface. A large formal pool like this is all the more effective for being perfectly still. The surrounding path is wide enough for a wealth of low-growing and alpine plants, some in pots and some planted in cracks within the paving. The whole feature is part of a larger garden pattern, forming the focal point of a sunken area of grass and planting.*

INFORMAL PONDS

Natural ponds are invariably informal. If you want to create something similar in your own garden you should first study how water looks without the interference of man. For a start, it will almost certainly be situated in a fold or dip in the land and, although we don't always have that much space at home, we can at least use the shapes and contours of the garden to ensure that the feature sits comfortably in its surroundings. You can use the spoil from the excavation for this contouring. Remember to keep the topsoil separate from the subsoil, replacing it last as a medium for planting or lawn.

Since natural ponds do not have any kind of artificial lining, one of the worst blunders in building an informal pool is to leave the edge of a butyl sheet or concrete rim projecting above the water. The secret is, of course, to lay the liner beneath the bank, bringing it up above the water level a short way from the edge of the pool. The sides of the pool should, if possible, dip gently towards the water with marginal planting linking the two elements together. Alternatively, a beach of cobbles or small stones can be a most effective edge and will allow animals to approach and drink more easily.

Planting is vitally important both in and around a natural pond. On a very grand scale, trees, and particularly weeping trees, will provide a strong vertical line against the horizontal plane of water. Willows are quite magnificent if you have a garden and lake of many acres but are a disaster in a small plot. Far better is weeping birch or one of the larger shrubs such as dogwood or bamboo.

I'm very much against the use of brash fountains in informal ponds. Reflections are far more telling: if a pool can be sited so that it mirrors a wide open sky or a particularly fine area of planting then your design is almost guaranteed to be a success. In a rural situation, you might even occasionally have the opportunity of using water as a boundary, drawing the more distant landscape into the garden. In this instance a fence becomes superfluous and you can enjoy that rare and precious element – an uninterrupted view of the open countryside beyond.

Opposite above: *One of the great joys of having a pool is being able to walk across it. Some bridges are pretentious and ghastly, an unfavourable reflection of the character of the owner. Far better, as here, to have a simple timber structure that is softened by the generous planting.*

Opposite below: *I suspect this pond started life as a formal composition, but somebody who loves plants has got hold of it and obliterated the geometric lines. To my mind this is the right approach: formality is there to be tempered – and what a haven this must be for wildlife.*

Right: *This stunning combination of irises and primulas provides a splash of vibrant colour against the darker background of shrubs. The banks of the pool disappear into the shadows whilst the lily pads provide shade and shelter for the fish and other pond life.*

RAISED POND

A raised pond is both an attractive and a practical feature in a garden, and this one is the perfect height to double as an occasional seat. However, as with all water features, safety must be paramount, and if you choose to build a pond then do make sure it is child-safe.

The pond shown here is 1800mm (72in) long, 1350mm (54in) wide and approximately 300mm (12in) high. The exterior surfaces are clad in slate, although you could use paving or natural stone materials; the important consideration is to match the cladding to the paving.

CONSTRUCTION
Prepare a sound base. On a solid concrete surface this will involve very little, but in the garden make sure that the surface is level and excavate suitable foundations or footings. These must be twice as wide as the walls and approximately 300mm (12in) deep. Check the depth of the footings all round and drive stakes into the bottom of the trench so that they are just below ground level, ensuring they are level. Fill the trench with concrete up to the height of the pegs.

230 × 230 × 460mm block

SETTING OUT THE BASE

Leave the concrete to set for two days, then skim off any soil that is standing proud of the foundations. Remove any sharp stones that could damage the pool liner.

Build the walls from a single course of hollow concrete blocks. Mark out the lines for these using chalk, checking the corners are at right angles using a 3:4:5 triangle. Build the pool to a size that avoids having to cut the blocks.

Lay a 10mm ($\frac{3}{8}$in) bed of mortar along one long side between chalk lines and lay a single course of blocks, with mortar between each. Check that the course is level and true. Remove any surplus mortar and ensure the joints are flush on the inside faces.

Repeat the process to lay the first course for both of the short sides and then the second long length.

Set out the cladding dry for each of the sides, allowing sufficient overlap at one end to butt the next side up to it. Work your way along the face of one side, then carry out any necessary cutting when you get to the corner. Set the cladding on to the face of the concrete blocks with mortar so that it finishes flush with the top. A crisp rectangular material, such as slate, can be closely butt jointed, but any joints that show should be neatly rubbed back.

OVERHEAD PLAN

Clean up the inside faces of the concrete blocks and remove any sharp protrusions or edges that could damage the butyl pond liner. Lay a sheet of liner underlay and fix in place with builders' tape.

Lay a 15mm ($\frac{5}{8}$in) layer of soft sand over the base of the pool to cushion the pond liner. The size of liner should be twice the depth of the pool plus the overall length, and twice the depth of the pool plus the overall width. Lay the liner over the pool walls, ease it into place and loosely hold with half a dozen slabs around the edges.

Fill the pool with water to within 25mm (1in) of the top. The liner will stretch and mould to the exact profile of the walls. Trim the excess liner to leave a 40mm (1$\frac{1}{2}$in) fringe that can be secured under the coping. Any wrinkles, should be folded so they lie flat.

The coping should be the same material as the cladding. Lay it out around the pool prior to bedding in the mortar so the coping can be cut to fit. The coping should overhang

the inside of the pond by 50mm (2in) to help hide the liner, and to cast a soft shadow.

Lay the coping on a 10mm ($\frac{3}{8}$in) bed of mortar. A useful precaution against the pond overflowing is to bed a section of 15mm ($\frac{5}{8}$in) diameter plastic pipe across the mortar, so that it runs between the inside and outside faces of one wall.

Lay the coping above the pipe, checking that it is level.

OVERFLOW DETAIL

Pipe

Coping

Liner

CROSS-SECTION OF POND

Coping

Liner

Block

ELEMENTS OF DESIGN

As in other parts of the garden, the overall concept and make-up of a pond can be split into the elements of hard and soft landscape. The method of construction and certain features will fall under the former while the planting, fish, insect and other life will follow on as a natural second stage to complement the size, position, materials and style chosen for the pool.

I have already mentioned the differences between concrete and liner construction, emphasizing the advantages of the latter being made from material that is better suited to prolonged contact with water.

In most instances, and certainly in formal pools, the liner will need anchoring in some way. This is usually done with a coping that surrounds the pool. The range of copings is wide but your choice should, if possible, take its cue from materials used elsewhere in the garden. If you have a terrace or patio constructed from stone slabs then your pool could use a similar coping. The same would apply to brick, slate or concrete paving. Preformed fibreglass pools should also be fitted with a coping to disguise the edge – brick often conforms best to the convoluted shapes of many of the free-form types. For durability and safety the coping should be securely bedded on mortar. If a pool is situated within a lawn area then the coping should be set slightly below the level of the turf so that a mower can run smoothly over the top.

Lighting can add an altogether new dimension to a pool at night. There are a number of easy-to-install kits available. Safety is of paramount importance, so if in doubt, employ the services of a qualified electrician. Some pool lighting is appalling, particularly the floating, rotating, multicoloured displays that seem designed to induce a migraine in double-quick time. Stick to white and blue bulbs, which are both the most natural and the most effective. Bulbs in these colours will enhance the appearance of the foliage growing in and around the water rather than detract from it, and can be used in conjunction with other areas of lighting around the garden. Simplicity and subtlety are the keys to success, otherwise the resulting illuminated scene will merely look contrived.

Lily pads are one of the most satisfying elements of a pond, but need water that is about 600mm (24in) deep. The more rampant varieties of lily will also require regular thinning.

Opposite above left: A well-balanced pool will always have frog potential and they should be encouraged. It's fascinating, particularly for children, to watch tadpoles develop, while adult frogs are an enormous help with pest control in the garden.

Opposite above right: Rock often associates well with water, but only if it is used in as natural a way as possible. Each piece should be set at the same angle, along a 'bedding plane'. Marginal planting, set in baskets on a shelf below the water, brings the composition to life and softens the somewhat austere rock backdrop.

Opposite below left: Fish are a vital ingredient in pond design, helping to provide a balanced environment as well as constant movement. Varieties range from the common goldfish to the exotic Coy carp. Be sure to seek specialist advice before you make your final choice.

Opposite below right: Lily flowers are among the most spectacular in the garden and the great waxy blooms will bring high drama to any pool. Because their colours are so vibrant you should choose them to blend with the surrounding planting schemes.

Right: *An old glazed sink has been covered with Hypatufa, a mixture of cement, adhesive and peat. This encourages the speedy growth of a layer of moss and lichen, mimicking the appearance of real stone and providing an interesting textured surface that blends well with the surrounding environment.*

Far right: *Half a barrel makes an excellent small pool, though it will be difficult to maintain an ecological balance to prevent stagnation if you are not prepared to clean and care for it regularly. The plants here are growing well but will need regular maintenance and thinning if they are not to overrun the area completely, becoming tangled and unrecognizable.*

SMALL-SCALE SOLUTIONS

Ponds can come in all shapes, sizes and containers, and need not necessarily be confined by conventional criteria. Having said that, the smaller the pool the more difficult it will be to maintain a balanced combination of plants and fish. Maintenance is often higher, particularly if fish are omitted, as unchecked weed and algal growth will need removing from time to time. It is worth remembering that even pools like this should not be completely emptied on a regular basis. What you should do is drain off about a quarter of the water each year, which will remove a percentage of the toxins, and replace with fresh. Lose any more than that and you will upset the ecological balance that has built up.

In some instances you may not want a conventional pool at all. If young children use the garden, an area of open water will present a real hazard. An alternative would be to set an old millstone or drilled boulder above a tank and pump water up and over it in a continuous cycle. This recreates the refreshing sound of moving water, is irresistible to children and, most importantly, is completely safe. A raised bed could well incorporate this idea, with planting, loose cobbles and other boulders to complete the picture. Although a number of manufacturers produce simulated millstones, they rarely look as good as the real thing. A much better idea is to hunt out just what you want, enjoying the satisfying knowledge that whatever you finally construct will be unique.

One water feature in my garden at home is a large cast-iron bath. It sits, ponderously, close to the french windows, surrounded by pots and containers of various sizes and is filled with water, fish and plants. There is even a plug for easy drainage! It is the quickest pond I have ever built and looks just fine. For me the most important point is that I derived a great deal more pleasure from doing something constructive with the bath than I would have done if I had simply

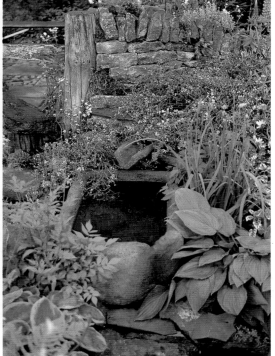

Far left: *This pool has a Japanese feel but rather lacks conviction. Nonetheless, the idea of using cobbles as a beach is an excellent one and can be adapted to suit pools of varying styles. The stream of water flowing down the slate steps between the planting contributes a feeling of harmony and provides a relaxing 'background noise' to peaceful activities in the garden.*

Left: *This is a real cracker of a stone sink, blending perfectly with the drystone wall and soft planting in a composition designed by Julian Dowle. Continuity and sensitivity have been blended into a harmonious whole – which is what good garden design is all about and which can be achieved with a combination of imagination and careful planning.*

broken it up and sent it down to the scrap yard.

Another eccentric pool I once designed was in an old boat. Again, this worked excellently, as a dinghy is equally equipped to keep water in as it is to keep it out. The composition was set in an informal part of the garden with the boat gently drifting out of a bed into the lawn. The inclusion of original and unexpected elements is one of the great strengths of good garden design – add humour to this and the picture is often complete.

Half a barrel filled with plants and water is a classic container for making into a small-scale pond. Make sure that the barrel did not previously contain wood preservative oil (the residue of which will contaminate the water), and scrub the inside of the barrel clean using water. Spread a layer of clean soil over the base of the barrel and mix with a little water into a slurry. Bed a few pond plants in the soil, then add a layer of fine shingle above the soil to keep the plants rooted in place. Fill the barrel with water almost to the rim, taking care not to disturb the soil. You will need to let the water settle and allow the temperature to stabilize for about a week before adding a few fish and some snails.

Not all ponds need to be built as a single unit, however, and you could consider split-level arrangements where one plane of water drops to the next, either by a simple waterfall or a water slide of some kind. A variation of this idea is a water staircase where a series of ponds drop down a slope. Some of the great Italian Renaissance gardens featured such staircases on an enormous scale. Today you could modify the idea and reduce it down to create a feature in a quite modest area. A sloping garden has perhaps the greatest potential for water which can be handled both formally and informally. A series of irregularly shaped pools linked by streams and falls and surrounded by planting will provide an entirely natural look, while crisply architectural sheets of water, worked into the angles of a flight of steps, create just the opposite effect. As long as the garden, or at least that part of the garden, embraces the overall theme, either approach would be entirely appropriate.

FOUNTAIN

Although water is one of the key elements in any garden it can present problems. Safety is an obvious consideration and so, too, is maintenance to keep the surface clear. This feature presents a negligible hazard to children, is easy to build and looks delightful throughout the year. In addition, it provides a real focal point as well as a cooling influence on a hot summer's day. The relatively small scale demands that it be positioned close to a terrace or in full view of a window; it could all too easily be lost in a more distant part of the garden or concealed altogether if poorly sited.

CONSTRUCTION

Strip the surface of the site of vegetation and mark out a circle with a radius of 600mm (24in) using a piece of string attached to a central stake to act as a compass. Carefully remove the topsoil within the circle to a depth of 75mm (3in).

Mark out a rectangle 600 × 450mm (24 × 18in) within the centre of the circle and dig this to a depth of 550mm (22in), extending slightly beyond the edges of the rectangle. Position a layer of hardcore, 75mm (3in) thick, at the bottom of the pit, ram it down and cover the finished surface with sand to remove any irregularities. The tank to be placed in the pit, which can be made from either galvanized steel or plastic, can now be lowered into the pit and the position adjusted so that the base is level. Position a strip of butyl pond liner, approximately

**MARKING OUT AND
EXCAVATING THE SITE**

300mm (12in) wide, around the rim
of the tank so that 150mm (6in)
hangs down on either side.

Carefully backfill soil around the
tank, firming this down as you
work. Grade the final slope up to
the circumference of the
surrounding circle, leaving two flat
ledges, 75mm (3in) wide, along the
600mm (24in) long sides of the tank
– these will support the foot-
scrapers. Cover the soil surface with
a thin layer of soft sand and fold the
liner hanging on the inside of the
tank back over the sand.

Cut another section of liner to form
a circle 75mm (3in) larger in
diameter than that marked on the
ground and cut a central hole
150mm (6in) within the perimeter of
the tank. Carefully lay this liner in
position over the site.

The fountain is driven by a
submersible, low-voltage pump
fitted with a head that will finish
just proud of the galvanized foot-
scrapers. Choose one with an output
of about 30l/min (400gal/hr). You
can adjust the height of the pump

by standing it on bricks or concrete
blocks built up within the tank.
Run the cable from the pump over
the liner. Use builders' tape to
fasten and protect the cable at the
point where it passes over the rim of
the tank.

Two galvanized foot-scrapers are
positioned on the prepared shelves
(one on each side of the
fountain head) to prevent the loose
boulders and pebbles falling into
the tank. Fit two offcuts of doubled
butyl pond liner over the shelves
underneath the scrapers to act as
cushions to the liner below.

During a hot summer, evaporation
when the fountain is working will
be considerable. A dip-stick is
essential for regular checks to the
water level within the tank. Cut a
tube for the stick to run through
from 20mm ($\frac{3}{4}$in) rigid PVC pipe to
reach from the bottom of the tank
to just above the level of the foot-
scrapers. Position the pipe vertically
and tie it back to a slat on the
scraper. Slide a bamboo cane down
the tube and clearly mark on it one
level 150mm (6in) above the level of

the pump and another 75mm (3in)
below the rim of the tank; you can
now use the cane to tell if the water
level drops to a dangerous level and
to check that you have topped up
the tank with water to an
appropriate level.

Use a hosepipe to fill the tank so
that the water level just covers the
pump. Run the cable back to the
house and connect it to the
transformer according to the
manufacturer's instructions. Any
outside wiring to the mains must be
carried out by a qualified
electrician. Test the system and the
pump for correct operation and

adjust the fountain pressure for the
height of spray you want. There is
normally a simple valve that you can
easily adjust to achieve this.

Position loose cobbles and small,
smooth boulders around the
circumference of the circle, and trim
off any excess pond liner that is
visible. Position the remainder of
the stones working from the centre
outwards, so that the whole area is
covered and there are no gaps
through which you can see the
pump mechanism in the tank below.
Fill the tank to the upper mark on
the dip-stick, switch on the power,
and enjoy the results!

CORNER DETAIL

PLAN VIEW

Above: Simplicity can achieve a great deal in visual terms. This concrete bowl is perfectly suited to its purpose as a birdbath. The tap is a practical idea and ensures that water is readily available.

Above right: An elaborate cast-iron or aluminium birdbath like this would be expensive, but is certainly elegant. Black is a good landscape colour and blends well with planting, but such a shallow bath would need topping up regularly in hot weather.

BIRDBATHS AND FOUNTAINS

Birdbaths and fountains provide the finishing touches to your garden, the final details that put charisma into the composition. As well as being ecologically sound, allowing not just birds but many other wild creatures to drink, birdbaths act as pretty focal points, drawing the eye in a particular direction.

Shapes and styles of birdbath vary enormously, from a basic wooden bowl set on the edge of a raised bed or wall to elaborate affairs cast in metal or hewn from stone. I believe that in all areas of design the simplest things work best and any feature should take its style from the area that surrounds it. The simplest birdbath might be a crevice set within a large rock, exactly right in an informal setting. The most complicated could be an ornate pattern in wrought-iron, perfectly at home in the formal setting of a crisp town garden while still fulfilling its function of attracting the local birdlife.

Birdbaths should be shallow and with gently sloping sides. If you or your neighbours have cats, then the birdbath should be set high enough to discourage cats from disturbing the birds. It is a good idea to line the bottom with coarse sand or gravel so that birds can get a foothold.

Fountains can be spectacular or simple, but should again suit the overall garden pattern. A huge jet needs to be in a huge pond some distance from the house or viewing point, whereas a small fountain will do much the same visual job closer to home. The height at which the jet is set will also play a part. If it spouts from the top of a bowl at eye-level, much of the effect will be lost when sitting down. This would be a composition to be viewed when walking, perhaps in a front garden on the way to the main entrance. Similarly a bubble jet, just breaking the surface of the water, will be most effective when sitting. Think about height, position and sound right at the beginning of the planning stages. It will certainly pay great dividends later on, when the fountain will be all the more appreciated if it can be seen to best advantage.

Left: *The delicious contrast between the formality of the fountain and the informality of the surrounding planting provides an excellent study in garden design. The pool is large enough to support both plants and a few small fish, while the arching sprays of water reflect the sunlight beautifully before falling past the bowl in the kind of shower that birds appreciate. Refreshing and pleasant to the eye and the ear, a fountain with a small pool is a welcome feature in a garden, and always contributes to a relaxing environment.*

DIRECTORY OF TECHNIQUES

LAYING A PATIO OF PAVING SLABS

Use pegs and string lines to mark out the area of the site according to the dimensions of the slabs so that, if possible, only whole slabs will be used. Allow for a consistent gap of 6–12mm ($\frac{1}{4}$–$\frac{1}{2}$in) between the slabs.

Excavate the site to a depth of 75–100mm (3–6in) according to how firm the ground is (the firmer the ground, the shallower the excavation can be). Ram down a layer of hardcore in the bottom two thirds of your excavation, checking with a spirit level that the surface is flat and level. Cover the hardcore with a thin layer of sand to fill any gaps.

The concrete slabs should be laid on a continuous layer of mortar. However, on a sufficiently firm surface, it will be easier to bed the slabs on spots of mortar. Starting in one corner of the site, put down five spots of mortar, about 38–50mm ($1\frac{1}{2}$–2in) deep and 75mm (3in) in diameter. Carefully align the slab with the string lines, and bed it on the mortar. Lay a short length of timber on the slab and tap down with a mallet until the slab is level. Use a spirit level to check that the crossfall and lengthways slope of the slab are even.

Using 6mm ($\frac{1}{4}$in) or 12mm ($\frac{1}{2}$in) plywood spacers, lay the first row of slabs, checking with a 3:4:5

triangle that the slabs are being laid square to the adjacent ones. You can make a 3:4:5 triangle from scrap wood: nail a 75mm (3in) length at right angles to a 100mm (4in) length, then nail a brace across the hypotenuse so that its length is exactly 125mm (5in) from corner to corner.

Move the string line along to mark the outside edge of the second row of slabs, then lay the two slabs at either end, again using spacers. Fill in the remaining slabs, then repeat until you have paved the whole area.

Remove the spacers after two days, then fill in the gaps with mortar, or leave them open for grass to grow through.

LAYING A PATH

The hardest-wearing paths are laid on a continuous layer of mortar. Whether the surfacing material is stone, concrete slabs, crazy paving or sections of hardwood, you should excavate the area just as for a patio, with a well-compacted layer of hardcore at the base. Again, bedding the material on generous spots of mortar is a simple task, and has the advantage of making it easier to lift them up should you need to reach any pipes buried beneath.

The simplest method, however, is to lay stepping stones across the lawn, setting them about 12mm ($\frac{1}{2}$in) below the level of the grass so that a mower can pass over.

LAYING PAVING SLABS

LAYING SLABS ON A LAYER OF MORTAR

LAYING SLABS ON SPOTS OF MORTAR

LAYING SLABS IN GRASS

STEPS FROM RAILWAY SLEEPERS
If the slope of the ground is not too steep, railway sleepers can be recessed into the soil and pegged in place to provide an informal flight of steps in a garden. Dig out troughs: these should be to the length of the sleeper, and about 12mm ($\frac{1}{2}$in) deep at the front and almost to the depth of the sleeper at the back. Ram the sleepers firmly in place and drive wooden stakes (thoroughly coated with non-toxic exterior-grade preservative) into the ground just in front of the sleepers to hold them in place. Place rocks between the treads for sculptural effect and grow plants at the sides to soften the edges.

For a slightly more formal and durable solution, railway sleepers can be combined with concrete slabs. In this case, the sleepers and the slabs must be bedded on a 50mm (2in) layer of mortar above a 150mm (6in) layer of well-compacted hardcore, which means that you will have to excavate the site first. Bed the sleepers as shown (below) so that the top of the sleeper is level with the top of the slab 'above' it. Tap the sleepers down with a mallet until they are level with the appropriate slabs, and check with a spirit level that the slabs themselves are not sloping. Take care that the sleeper does not protrude above the concrete slab.

STEPS FROM BRICKS AND CONCRETE SLABS
The formal steps shown here are built up from ground level to a raised platform or patio of concrete slabs, rather than being built into an existing slope. They rest firmly in place above layers of hardcore, concrete and mortar. This design might be useful if you want a hard-surfaced area above the patio area.

Measure the height difference between the upper and lower levels, and calculate how many treads (the concrete slabs) and risers (the bricks) you will require. Here, the small step only requires a riser from the ground level to the tread, and then a second riser to take one up to the upper level.

Excavate according to the slope and lay well-compacted hardcore. Dig a trench 300mm (12in) deep to support the first riser and fill it with about 25mm (1in) of hardcore. Fill the rest of the trench with concrete, tamp it down flat, cover and leave for three days. Bed a row of bricks to the width of the step on a 50mm (2in) layer of mortar, then lay a concrete slab above it so that it protrudes beyond the riser by about 25mm (1in). Ensure the tread is level, and then bed the next row of brick risers. Continue until you have built the steps to the required height.

RAILWAY SLEEPERS

BRICKS AND CONCRETE SLABS

RAILWAY SLEEPERS AND CONCRETE SLABS

BUILDING A BRICK WALL

It is important to lay secure foundations when building a brick wall. Failure to do so will lead to rapid subsidence and collapse. The length and depth of foundations must vary according to the height of the construction; but if you are in doubt it is wise to be generous.

Anything higher than a low brick planter will need purpose-built, solid concrete foundations which should be twice the width of the wall. A single brick thickness wall, up to 1000mm (39in) high, will require a trench 350–400mm (14–16in) deep. Into this, lay a 150mm (6in) deep level bed of concrete (one part cement to four parts ballast). The foundations then should be left to harden for four days and should

be protected from the elements by covering in plastic during rain, or in damp sacking during hot weather. The sack should be sprayed with water to prevent the foundations cracking.

In addition to firm foundations, for a wall to be stable, it is advisable to have piers (support columns) at both ends.

Once the foundations are ready, use string lines to act as a guide when you lay the first course of bricks. Set up profile boards with notches at the appropriate width for the wall either end of the trench and insert the string in the notches; this will hold it taut.

Next, spread a layer of mortar on the concrete bed. The mortar should be just over 10mm ($\frac{3}{8}$in) thick, bearing in mind that it will be compressed slightly by the

application of the bricks. Set the first brick in place, indentation or 'frog' upwards, at one end of the mortar. The next brick should be laid about 1220mm (48in) away. To ensure that they are level, place a spirit level on a piece of wood bridging the two bricks and gently tap down the higher one with a trowel handle until they are level. Repeat for every brick in the first course, 'buttering' each brick end with mortar to form the vertical joints.

Vertical joints must be staggered, so the second course should be started with a brick cut in half. To do this, cut a groove right round a brick with a bolster chisel and hammer, lay it on a bed of sand, insert the chisel in the groove and tap sharply with the hammer to get a clean cut.

The ends of the wall should be built up three or four courses ahead of the course being completed. Each course must be laid to a taut string line, pinned into the course above the one you are laying.

As you build the wall you should check regularly with a length of wood marked with the height of each course that they are accurate, and that the face of the brickwork is even. As each course is completed, finish the joints by removing excess mortar with the edge of a trowel. These are known as flush joints; rounded joints are achieved by rubbing back the mortar with a piece of hosepipe or bucket handle. Lay the top course (the coping course) of bricks on edge to protect the wall from the worst of the weather.

Damp course

Pier

String line

PROFILE OF A BRICK WALL

BUILDING A BRICK WALL

FIXING POSTS

Metal post spikes can be driven into soil and the post fitted into the square cup above the earth. Alternatively a post hole borer can be driven into the ground and then removed with the displaced earth. Fill the bottom of the hole with well-compacted hardcore, insert the post, and fill around with concrete, sloping it away from the post to allow better drainage.

On concrete or paving stones, you can use a steel base as the fixing point. The square plate can be bolted in place and the post inserted in the projecting cup. Alternatively, the bolt or bracket can be cemented into the paving and the post fitted into it. Another method is to chip through the surface of the patio or paving stones and then concrete the post in place without using a bracket. Always check the posts for vertical, adjust as necessary and treat with non-toxic preservative.

FIXING TRELLIS PANELS

Trellis is often secured to walls, but an alternative if this is not feasible or desirable is to use vertical support posts. Having fixed these in the ground at the necessary distance apart (the spacing will depend on the width of the trellis of fence panels), place bricks or blocks on the ground to support the panels at the required height above the ground. To avoid the panels rotting at the bottom, trellis should be fixed at least 150mm (6in) above ground level. Metal, purpose-made clips (panel brackets) can then be nailed into the posts at a suitable level. For panels up to 1800mm (72in) high, you will require three clips per side. Ensure that the clips are at the same height on each post and inset by the same amount. Lift the panels into place, making sure that the horizontal rails of the panels are level. Fix the panels to the clips using zinc-plated or brass screws.

PICKET FENCE

POST AND RAIL FENCE

PANEL FENCE

FIXING POSTS

FIXING TRELLIS

TYPES OF FENCING

The variety of styles of fencing mean that there is certain to be one that suits your garden perfectly.

Picket fences, with their pointed or rounded tops, are usually about 900mm (36in) high, and are used to define a boundary, usually at the front of a house. Traditionally painted white, there's no reason why you shouldn't add a splash of colour if the fancy takes you.

Post and rail fences definitely look best in a country setting, since they don't provide much in the way of privacy or protection, but do allow marvellous views of the scenery beyond. They are stock-proof, and gates should be of the five-bar type. Alternatively, you can build a stile that will allow you to cross over the fence with ease.

Panel fences are quite expensive, especially if your boundary is quite large, but they are easy to install. They provide the best degree of privacy and weather protection, although used at the front of the house they look rather hostile. A large expanse of panel fence is not the most attractive of sights: the best thing is to plant some fast-growing climbers against the panel to provide a more attractive view.

ABOVE: CORNER HALVING JOINT; BELOW: CROSS HALVING JOINT

Streichmaß

CUTTING A 'T'-HALVING JOINT

WOOD JOINTS

In order to ensure that anything you build in the garden is strong and secure, it is essential that you join various pieces of work accurately. The joints described here will be useful in building many of the projects featured in this book. Although it is important to measure the dimensions accurately, don't be deterred by striving for an absolutely perfect finish: one of the joys of building wooden structures in the garden is that they will mellow with age, and will often have plants growing up and around them. For this reason, the quality of the finish does not need to be as fine as if you were making a piece of furniture for use indoors. However, it is a good idea to practise cutting joints on some pieces of scrap wood first.

CUTTING A BUTT JOINT

This is the simplest woodworking joint of all. The edge of one piece of wood is butted up against the side or face of another piece of wood, and fastened in place with glue. The joint is normally further reinforced using nails or corrugated fasteners.

It is important that the faces of the pieces of wood to be joined are cut or planed square so that they butt together neatly.

A variation on the butt joint is the mitre joint, in which the edges or faces of the two pieces of wood to be joined are cut at an angle and then butted together. Usually, the angle is cut at 45 degrees, so that the pieces of wood form a right angle when joined. However, they can be cut to any angle, as is the case with the fascia boards for the arbour project.

CUTTING A HALVING JOINT

Halving joints are used to join two pieces of wood of similar dimensions. The joint requires both pieces of wood to be cut through half their thickness (hence the name). There are three variations of the joint, according to where the two pieces of wood are being jointed: a corner halving joint joins two pieces of wood at their ends; a 'T'-halving joint joins the end of one board to a point anywhere along the length of the other piece of wood; and a cross-halving joint is formed when the faces of two pieces of wood are jointed to meet along their lengths.

Mark on each piece of wood the width of the cut-out (that is, the width of the other piece of wood), using a try square to make sure that it is square. Transfer the

lines of the cut-out to the edges of the timber and, with a marking gauge set to half the thickness of the piece of wood, mark the depth of the cut-out. Hold the piece of work in a vice and, using a tenon saw, carefully cut down the marked lines to the depth of the joint (half the thickness of the piece of wood), then carefully chisel out the waste wood.

If you are sawing a corner halving joint, then you will be measuring in for the thickness of the joint from the end of the piece of wood. In this case, first cut down the marked line to the depth of the joint; next, turn the piece of wood on end (so that it is upright) and replace it firmly in the vice. You can now carefully saw down the length of the joint, again using a tenon saw. Any rough edges can be sanded.

CUTTING A HOUSING JOINT

Stech-
beitel

CUTTING A NOTCH JOINT

CUTTING A HOUSING JOINT

A housing joint is essentially a slot into which the end of a piece of wood fits at right angles.

Mark the width of the slot (that is, the width of the piece of wood that will be joined) across the wide face of the piece of wood into which it will be cut. Use a try square for this, and extend the lines over on to the edges of the piece of wood.

The slot should be cut to a depth that is half the thickness of the piece of wood. Use a marking gauge to mark the depth between the marked lines on the edges.

Score across the lines marking the width of the slot so that you can locate the blade of the saw more easily, and cut down to the depth of the joint using a tenon saw. Chisel out the waste wood, working in from both edges.

CUTTING A BARE-FACED HOUSING JOINT

This is used to join the corners of a frame, and is very strong because a notch in the corner of one piece of wood is held in the housing cut into the other piece. When cutting this joint, the end of the piece of wood in which the housing is cut should be left overlong; the excess wood is then cut off neatly, flush with the top of the joint once the tongue has been nailed in place.

Mark out and cut the housing to a depth of between one third and half the thickness of the wood. On the other piece, mark out a tongue so that it will fit snugly in the housing. The tongue should be no less than half the wood's thickness. Join the two pieces so the tongue is on the underside of the corner.

CUTTING A NOTCH JOINT

A notch joint is like a mortise and tenon joint, except that the mortise (slot) is cut in the top of one of the pieces of wood into which the tenon (tongue) fits.

Mark out the tenon centrally on the end of one of the pieces of wood to about one third the thickness of the wood. The length of the tenon should be the width of the other piece of wood. Mark this distance down from the end and square the line around all four faces. Use a tenon saw to cut down the length of the tongue, then saw across the sides to remove the rest of the waste.

Mark the width of the slot on the end of the other piece of wood to correspond to the width of the tenon. Use a tenon saw to cut down to the depth of the slot, then neatly chisel out the waste.

CUTTING A REBATE

A rebate is an L-shaped cut along the end or edge of a piece of wood to accommodate another piece at right angles to it. Sometimes, a rebate is cut in both pieces so that they slot together.

Mark the rebate along the end or length of the piece of wood. Its width should be the thickness of the piece of wood that is going to be joined to it; its depth should not exceed half of the width. If you are cutting rebates in both pieces of wood, their width and depth should be half the thickness of the wood.

Cramp the piece of wood and cut down to the width of the rebate using a tenon saw. Lay the piece of wood down flat and cut down to the depth of the rebate. If the rebate is very shallow, you may prefer to chisel out the waste.

INDEX

Page numbers in *italic* refer to illustrations and captions.

acid soils, 10
alkaline soils, 10
arbours, 8, *38, 40, 47, 47*
    constructing, 48–51, *48–51*
arches, 8, *8,* 55
aspect, planning, 10

barbecues, *11, 32*
    construction, 34–5, *34–5*
    position, 13
bark chippings, 23
barrels, small pools, *82*
baths, 82
bean bags, 41
bean supports, 64, *64–5*
benches, *12*
birdbaths, 86, *86*
box, *72, 75*
bricks:
    paths, 21, *21,* 55
    paving, 14, *20,* 21, *21*
    raised beds, 67, *67*
    steps, *89*
    walls, 69, *69, 90*
bridges, *21, 76*

cascades, 74
chairs, 41
children in the garden, 31, 55, 66
chippings:
    stone, 23
    wood, 23
climbing plants, 18, *38,* 57–8, *59,*
    62, *62–3*
cobbles, 18, *24*
colour:
    fences, *12*
    screens, *55*
concrete:
    blocks, 54
    slabs, 89
containers, pots, *30,* 31
cottage gardens, *55*
courtyards, *10, 21*
creosote, 26

deck chairs, 41
decking, *27–9, 28–9*
dividers, 53–69
    making, 60–1
dovecots, 14
Dowle, Julian, *83*
drawings, preparing, 13
drives, materials, 14
eating outdoors, *30, 32–5,* 33, 34
electricity:
    lighting, 33
    pumps, 74
entrances, 8, *8*
    gates, *54–5,* 68, 69
fences, 69, *69, 93, 93*
    colour, *12*
    picket, *12*
figures, pools, 74
fish, 71, 72, *77,* 80, *80*
fountains, *72, 72, 74, 75,* 86, *87*
    construction, 84, *84–5*
foxgloves, *54*
fragrant plants, 33
frogs, *80*
fuchsias, *55*
furniture:
    colour, *32,* 41
    plastic, 41
    seating, 37–47
    wicker, *30, 32,* 47

gates, *54–5,* 68, 69
gazebo, *9, 32*
granite setts, 14, *18,* 24, *24*
gravel, 14
    paths, *17,* 22–3, *22, 23*
    patios, *19,* 22–3, *32*
hammocks, *40,* 41
hard landscaping, 14
hedges, *12,* 55, 68, 69
honeysuckle, *40*

ivy, *69*

Japanese gardens, 22, 23, *73*

lawns, sloping, 10
levels, changes in, 10
lighting, patios, 33
logs:
    raised beds, 26–7, 67
    seating, 38, *39*
    stepping stones, 27
    steps, 26, *27,* 89, *89*
long gardens, 8, *9*

McMahon, Hilary, 23
marble, 24
materials:
    paths, 17–27
    patios, 14, 17–27
    paved areas, 14
    pools, 72
meals outside, *30, 32–5,* 33, 34
measuring sites, 8
mystery, creating, *15*

natural pools, 76

ornaments, pools, 74

paths:
    brick, *20,* 21, *21,* 55
    edging, 22
    granite setts, *18*
    gravel, *17,* 22–3, *22, 23*
    laying, 88, *88*
    materials, 14, 17–27
    stone, 24, *24–5*
patios, *30–1,* 31
    brick, *20,* 21, *21*
    decking, 27–9
    gravel, *19,* 22–3, *32*
    laying, 88, *88*
    lighting, 33
    marble, 24
    materials, 14, 17–27
    pools, 72
    shape, 18
    siting, 13
    size, 18
    stone, 24, *24–5*

paving:
   brick, 14, 15, *15*
   materials, 17–27
   slate, 24, *24–5*
paving slabs:
   barbecue construction, *35*
   laying, 88, *88*
paviors, 14, 21
pergolas, 8, *8*, *9*, 15, 62, *62–5*
planning, 8–15
   design, 13–15
   drawings, 13
   hard landscaping, 14
   planting, 15
   surveying, 8–11
planting, design, 15
plants:
   climbing, 18, *38*, 57–8, *59*, 62, *62–3*
   pools, 76
   scented, 33
   softening effects, 14, 15, *15*, 18, *41*
   within paths, 22
plastic:
   furniture, 41
   pool liners, 72, 76
   trellis, 57
play areas, 31
ponds *see* pools
pools, *11*, 14, *71*
   bridges, *76*
   elements of design, 80
   formal, 74, *74–5*
   informal, 76, *76–7*
   liners, 72, 76
   natural, 76
   positioning, 13, 72
   raised ponds, 78–9, *78–9*
   reflections, 15, *75*, 76
   seating around, 38, *71*
   small scale, 82–3, *82–3*
   split level, 83
   wildlife, 71, 72, *77*, 80, *80*

porches, *59*
posts, fixing, 91, *91*
pots, *30*, *31*
preservatives, 26
projects:
   arbour, 48–51, *48–51*
   barbecue, 34–5, *34–5*
   bean support, 64–5, *64–5*
   decking, 28–9, *28–9*
   fountain, 84–5, *84–5*
   garden divider, 60–1, *60–1*
   raised ponds, 78–9, *78–9*
   tree seat, 42–5, *42–5*
pumps, fountains, 74
pyrus, *46*

railway sleepers, 26
   raised beds, 67
   seating, 38
   steps, 89, *89*
raised beds, *11*, 15, *31*, 66, *78–9*
   as dividers, 55
   log supported, 26–7
raised ponds, 78–9, *78–9*
reflections, pools, 15, *75*, 76
retaining walls, 10
rock, pool design, *80*
rockeries, 66
roof gardens, *11*, *30*, 31, 55, 59
   containers, 67
roses, 62, *63*

sandpits, 31
scaled drawings, 13
scented plants, 33
seating, 15, *15*, 37–47
   chairs, 41
   plastic, 41
   under trees, *37*, 41, 42–5, *42–5*
secret garden, *9*
shade, sitting areas, *40*, 41, 47
shrubs:
   positioning, 15
   topiary, *12*, 69
simplicity, *7*, 57

sinks, small pools, *83*
slate paving, 24, *25*
soil types, 10
spouts, water, 74
square gardens, 11
stepping stones, *15*, 24, 27
steps, *9*, 10
   brick, 89, *89*
   decking, 29
   railway sleeper, 89, *89*
   timber, 26, *27*
stone:
   paths, 24, *24–5*
   patios, 24, *24–5*
   reconstituted, 54
   seating, 38
stone chippings, 23
summer houses and gazebos, *9*, *32*
sun, sitting areas, 41, 47
sundials, 17, *20*
surveying, 8
swings, 55
terraces *see* patios
timber:
   decking, 28–9, *28–9*
   decorative screens, 54–5
   paths, 26–7, *27*
   patio surfaces, 26–7, *26*
   raised beds, 67, *67*
   seating, 38
   trellis, 57
   wood joints, 92–3, *92–3*
topiary, *12*, 69
trees:
   hammocks, 40, *41*
   positioning, 15
   seating under, *37*, 41, 42–5, *42–5*
   shade, 47
   topiary, *12*, 69
   weeping, 76
trellis, *53*, 54, 56–9, *57–8*
   fixing, 91, *91*
triangular gardens, 15
trompe-l'oeil, *57*

utility areas, play areas, 55

views, 10

walls, 54
   brick, 69, *69*, 90, *90*
   windows, *15*
water features, 8, *14*, 71–87
   bridges, *21*, 76
   patios, 18, *19*
   reflections, *15*, *75*, 76
   small-scale, 82–3, *82–3*
   wildlife, 71, 72, *77*, 80, *80*
   see also fountains, pools
water lilies, *77*, 80
water spouts, 74
weeping trees, 76
wicker furniture, *30*, *32*, 47
wildlife, 33, 71, 72
   pools, 71, 72, *77*, 80, *80*
willows, 76
windows, *15*
winds, 10
   windbreaks, 10, 58
winter gardens, *54*
wood *see* timber
wood chippings, 23

ACKNOWLEDGMENTS

The publisher thanks the following photographers and organisations for their permission to reproduce the pictures in this book:

1 Yves Duronsoy; 2–3 background Brigitte Thomas; 2 above left Jerry Harpur (designer Christopher Masson); 2 above right Ron Sutherland/Garden Picture Library; 2 below left Karen Bussolini; 2 below right Ron Sutherland/Garden Picture Library; 4 left Karen Bussolini; 4 centre Friedrich Strauss (Horst Schummelfeder); 4 right Edifice/Lewis; 4–5 Michael Boys/Boys Syndication; 5 left Karen Bussolini; 5 centre S&O Mathews; 5 right Michael Boys/Boys Syndication; 6–7 Camera Press; 8 Jerry Harpur (designer Michael Balston); 9 Brigitte Thomas (Erwan Tymen); 10–11 Brigitte Thomas (Erwan Tymen); 11 Jerry Harpur/Conran Octopus (architect John Burgee, garden Gwen Burgee with Tim Du Val); 12–13 Karen Bussolini; 13 Linda Burgess/Insight Picture Library; 14 Jerry Harpur (designer Ernie Taylor/Great Barr. West Midlands); 15 S&O Mathews; 16–17 Michael Boys/Boys Syndication; 18 Brigitte Thomas/Garden Picture Library; 19 Friedrich Strauss (Horst Schummelfeder); 20–21 background Linda Burgess/Insight Picture Library; 20 above left Jerry Harpur (designer Arabella Lennox-Boyd); 20 above right Jerry Harpur (designers Julie Toll & John Chambers. R.H.S. Chelsea 1991); 20 below left Jerry Harpur (Hazleby House, Berkshire); 20 below right Jerry Harpur/Conran Octopus; 22 above Jerry Harpur (designer Tim Newbury for Cramphorns P.L.C. R.H.S. Chelsea 1991); 22 below Karen Bussolini; 23 Jerry Harpur (designer Hilary McMahon. Costins Nursery. R.H.S. Chelsea 1991); 24–25 background Friedrich Strauss; 25 above left Jerry Harpur (designer Bruce Kelly, New York); 25 above right Friedrich Strauss (Horst Schummelfeder); 25 below S&O Mathews; 26 Jerry Harpur ('Dolwen' Llanrhaedr-ym-Mochnant); 27 Ron Sutherland/Garden Picture Library; 28 Eric Crichton; 30 Christopher Sykes; 30 right Brigitte Thomas (Timothy Vaughan); 31 above Jerry Harpur/Conran Octopus; 31 below Jerry Harpur (designer Ann Alexander Sinclair); 32 left Karen Bussolini; 32 above right Brigitte Thomas (Diana Humelen); 32 below right Ron Sutherland/Garden Picture Library; 33 above Friedrich Strauss (Horst Schummelfeder); 33 below Karen Bussolini; 34 Karen Bussolini; 36–37 Brigitte Thomas (Walda Pairon); 38 Andrew Lawson; 39 Michael Boys/Boys Syndication; 40 above Jerry Harpur ('Dolwen' Llanrhaedr-ym-Mochnant); 40 below Brigitte Thomas; 40–41 Friedrich Strauss (Horst Schummelfeder); 42 John Heseltine; 46 Andrew Lawson; 47 above John Glover/Garden Picture Library; 47 below Hugh Palmer; 48 Jerry Harpur; 52–53 Michael Boys/Boys Syndication; 54 left S&O Mathews; 54 right S&O Mathews; 55 left Christopher Sykes; 55 right Jerry Harpur/Conran Octopus (architect John Burgee, garden Gwen Burgee with Tim Du Val); 56–57 background Andrew Lawson; 56 above left Hugh Palmer; 56 above right John Ferris; 56 below left Karen Bussolini; 56 below right Brigitte Thomas (Erwan Tymen); 58–59 Jean-Paul Bonhommet; 59 above Jerry Harpur/Conran Octopus; 59 below John Heseltine; 60 Friedrich Strauss; 62 Jerry Harpur/Elizabeth Whiting & Associates (Gail Jenkins. Melbourne); 63 S&O Mathews; 64 Ron Sutherland (The Mien Ruys Garden, Holland)/Garden Picture Library; 66 above left Jerry Harpur (designer Douglas Knight/Formby Lancashire); 66 above right Eric Crichton (Peter Aldington); 66 below Friedrich Strauss; 67 S&O Mathews; 68 Edifice/Lewis; 69 above Peter Woloszynski; 69 below Jerry Harpur/Elizabeth Whiting & Associates (Sir Peter & Lady Finley. Sydney.); 70–71 Richard Bryant/Arcaid; 72 Jerry Harpur (Lower Hall Worfield/Salop, designed by Lanning Roper); 73 Ron Sutherland/Garden Picture Library; 74 above Friedrich Strauss (Horst Schummelfeder); 74 below Linda Burgess/Insight; 75 above David Russell/Garden Picture Library; 75 below John Miller; 76 above Friedrich Strauss (Landscape architect Neuberger); 76 below John Miller; 77 S&O Mathews; 78 Ron Sutherland/Garden Picture Library; 80–81 background Robert O'Dea; 81 above left John Miller; 81 below left Michael Boys/Boys Syndication; 81 above right Jack Townsend/Insight; 81 below right Michael Boys/Boys Syndication; 82 left Ron Sutherland/Garden Picture Library; 82 right Steven Wooster/Garden Picture Library; 83 left Jerry Harpur (designer Keith Gott, Japanese Garden Co. R.H.S. Chelsea 1991); 83 right Ron Sutherland/Garden Picture Library; 84 Eric Crichton (Mrs Fuller); 86 Ron Sutherland/Garden Picture Library; 87 Linda Burgess/Insight Picture Library.